TOY DOGS
A Comprehensive History And Guide to Modern Dogs

OTHER BOOKS AVAILABLE OR IN PRODUCTION

BREED BOOKS
The Bulldog - A Monograph by Edgar Farman
20th Century Bulldog by Marjorie Barnard, President, Bulldog Club
Hungarian Vizsla by Gay Gottlieb
Keeshond of the World by Margo Emerson
Staffordshire Bull Terrier in History and Sport by Mike Homan
The Bullmastiff by Clifford L B Hubbard
The Butterfly Dog by Clarice Waud and Pat Challis
The German Shepherd Dog by Joyce Ixer
The Dalmation by Clifford L B Hubbard
The Versatile Border Collie by Barbara Beaumont
Staffordshire Bull Terriers - Editor V C Hollender

GENERAL DOG BOOKS
Concise Guide to Dog Showing by Paddy Petch
The Dog Book by Betty Penn-Bull
Small Dog Obedience Training by Mrs R A Foreman
Pedigree Dogs in Colour. Official Standards and Colour Illustrations - Roy Hodrien

TOY DOGS

A Comprehensive History And Guide
to Modern Dogs
by
Clarice Waud
and
Mark Hutchings

NIMROD PRESS LTD.

ALTON,

HANTS

ISBN 1-85259-029-7

Typeset by:
Betagraphics, The King's House, Bow Street, Langport,
Somerset TA10 9PS

Printer: Ptarmigan Printing

NIMROD PRESS LTD.,
15 The Maltings,
Turk Street, Alton, Hants.

CONTENTS

Acknowledgements

This book would not have been possible without the help and assistance provided by many people, who either supplied information or photographs or both, and they are listed below. We are extremely grateful to them.

Affenpinscher	Mrs. T. Teasdale
Australian Silky Terrier	Mrs. D. Banks of the Australian Silky Terrier Club of New South Wales and Mrs. Colleen Mitchell of New South Wales, Australia.
Bichon Frise	Mrs. J. Ransom and Mr. M. Coad
Cavalier King Charles Spaniel	Mrs. D Schilizzi, Miss Betty Miller and Mrs. Montgomery, (U.S.A.)
Chihuahua	Mr. B. Leonard
Chinese Crested Dog	Mrs. M Hazelman, Mr. and Mrs. B. P. Jones and Mrs. B. Boxhall-James
English Toy Terrier (Black & Tan)	Mrs. S. Edwards and Mrs. H. Chamberlain
Griffon Bruxellois	Mrs. A. V. Fenn, Mrs. D. Kirk and Mr. S. Dangerfield
Italian Greyhound	Mrs. Annette Oliver and Mrs. S. Vincent
Japanese Chin	Miss Betty Miller
Lowchen	Mrs. F. McGregor
Maltese	Mrs. M. E. Lewin
Miniature Pinscher	Mr. F. J. Leonard
Pekingese	Mr. & Mrs. J. Mitchell, Mrs. Elenore Chaya and Mr. D. Roy
Yorkshire Terrier	Mr. O. A. Sameja

In addition the photographers Thomas Fall, Marc Henrie ASC and others provided photographs for us to choose suitable examples of the various breeds and Mary Evans of the Mary Evans Picture Library, Blackheath, provided us with some interesting early pictures which we have used. The book would not have been the same without their help.

INTRODUCTION

This book aims to give an insight into those breeds of dogs which are currently registered at the Kennel Club London, as toy dogs. The one exception is the now extinct Clydesdale Terrier, which is included because of its influence in the creation of the Yorkshire Terrier.

We endeavour to give some of the less generally known information about the early history of each breed, much of it quoted from some of the rarer antiquarian dog books. We also give the reader an idea of the general character and personality of each breed together with brief details of the basic care and attention required.. More detailed information of this aspect can be sought from specific books on each breed. The only breed we describe which appears to have no British monograph at the present time is the Lowchen, but it is now included in most of the modern books on dogs.

A feature of the book is the Toy Dog Bibliography which is the only comprehensive one as far as we know, devoted exclusively to the toy dog.

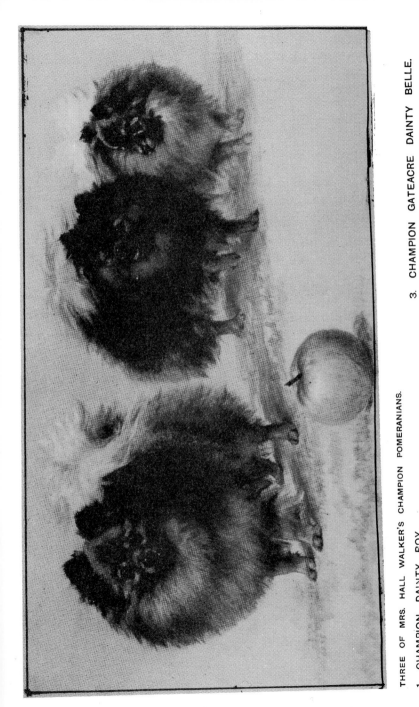

THREE OF MRS. HALL WALKER'S CHAMPION POMERANIANS.

1. CHAMPION DAINTY BOY.

2. CHAMPION GATEACRE BIBURY BELL.

3. CHAMPION GATEACRE DAINTY BELLE.

FROM THE PAINTING BY MAUD EARL.

Chapter 1

TOY DOGS AT COURT

For centuries Toy dogs have enjoyed Royal patronage, not only at the Courts in Europe. In Ethiopia the late Emperor, Haile Selassie, was devoted to animals of all sorts and many breeds of dogs were found at this Court. He was keenly interested in toy dogs, notably Chihuahuas and Papillons. His first Papillon was a coronation gift from the King of Italy in 1930. For some time he was exiled from his country, but when he returned in 1945 he had several Papillons with him on all occasions. Later he sent an agent to England to purchase and import more toy dogs.

In later chapters we describe in some detail the early popularity in their own countries of the Japanese Chin and the Pekingese and how the Japanese dogs were sent as gifts to the Courts of Portugal, Spain and Italy. We believe both these breeds originated in the Far East, and over the years there was considerable demand for them as gifts from the royalty of one country to another. The difficulty of obtaining Pekingese from the Imperial Palace in Pekin is legendary and many of the first dogs brought to England came as presents to the Royal Household and members of the aristocracy.

In Europe there is no doubt that the popularity of toy dogs increased as a result of the interest shown in them by the Royal families and nobility.

A century before the King Charles Spaniel appeared at the English Court, as the particular pet of Charles II, small dogs of this type were popular at the French Court and the northern town of Lyons was famous as their breeding place.

Sully, one of Henri III's Ministers and an eminent historian, wrote *The Popular History of France* and recorded details of the reign with care. He described the King's journey to Lyons "to buy little dogs" which were known as the chiens lyons, doubtless after the town from which they came. Henri was said to have a very large collection of dogs of various kinds and to have spent more than 100,000 crowns a year on their care, employing many servants for that purpose alone.

Sully did not have a high opinion of his master, stating that:

"Henri III possessed all the vulgar and low tastes."

This was a statement endorsed by other historians including H. A. L. Fisher in *A History of Europe* (1936) in which he described the King as a "degenerate who relied a great deal upon his powerful mother, Catherine de Medici".

In an article by V-R. de Bettex, entitled "Chiens gentilhommes" which appeared in *Bulletin des Courses*, is a picture by Ch. Hermann-Leon that shows the King sitting on a chair with his feet on a cushion and around his neck is a basket with three little dogs. At his feet is a large hound, a terrier is standing on its hind legs begging, a bichon lies under the chair and a small spaniel is eating from a dish on the floor. The King was said to favour jewellery and he is wearing the customary earring. It was a time of great stress in France and there is no doubt that the King, devoted to his pets, spent time and money on his hobby at the expense of the affairs of State. At such a time when the country was burdened with a heavy deficit which passed to his successor the Huguenot King Henri IV, it was perhaps not surprising that the King's preoccupation with his dogs did not endear him to some of his subjects any more than those of Charles II.

According to history King Charles II of England was particularly fond of small spaniels and in the chapter on King Charles Spaniels we refer to the comments of the two diarists of that time, Samuel Pepys and John Evelyn.

In the detailed diary in which Pepys set down daily events, however trivial, the spaniels were referred to on several occasions. John Evelyn's comments were mostly confined to affairs of State and to his charitable works, but his record in August 1662 is interesting to read:

"I dined with the Vice-Chamberlaine, and then went to see the Queen Mother, who was pleas'd to give me many thanks for the entertainment she receive'd at my house, when she recounted to me many observable stories of the sagacity of some dogs she formerly had."

We can imagine just such a conversation taking place today.

Evelyn, writing in 1685 soon after the death of King Charles said of him:

"He took delight in having a number of little spaniels follow him and lie in his bed-chamber, where he often suffer'd the bitches to puppy and give suck, which render'd it very offensive and indeed made the whole Court nasty and stinking."

This love of animals was shared by the King's successor, James II, but there has been no evidence that his dogs took up the King's time to the detriment of his affairs of State.

In the Scandinavian countries toy dogs, particularly toy spaniels, Pugs (known as "Mops") and Papillons, were also in evidence at Court. D. K. Ehrenstrahl painted portraits of the Royal Family with their pets. One can be found in Gripsholm Castle, Sweden which depicts a dog belonging to Queen Hedvig Eleonora of Sweden. It was called *Courtisane*, a very pretty toy spaniel, painted with a black and white companion. The Queen owned several toy spaniels and pictures by Ehrenstrahl include the black and white *Dondon* and a bitch called *Nespelina*.

A delightful picture of Prince Sigismund of Sweden, later King of Sweden and Poland, by an unknown painter and dated 1668, shows the Prince with a spaniel sitting at his feet.

In Denmark Princess Ulrica Eleonora of Denmark imported a toy spaniel from Bologna for which she paid the high price of 560 crowns. Her portrait with the dog was painted by Abraham Wuchters in 1679. The dog was tiny, lightly marked and had a pretty head with a thin narrow white blaze. Later the Princess became the wife of King Charles XI of Sweden.

So many of the toy breeds have been pets of the aristocracy. Pugs, Italian Greyhounds, Maltese, Bichons in Europe, King Charles and Cavaliers, Japanese, Pekingese and others. We think most were the pets of the ladies, although there are well known exceptions to this supposition. It is probable that, had it not been for the patronage of Royalty and the aristocracy in the dim past, there would not now be twenty toy breeds registered with the Kennel Club. Many breeds of "toie" dog, a definition which dates back many centuries, might not have survived to enjoy their present day popularity.

1.1 The Toy Dog Show at the Westminster Aquarium. 1887.

The following chapters on individual breeds will explain more fully their origins and subsequent progress over the centuries.

1.2 Toy spaniels owned by Queen Hedvig Eleonora. Copy after a painting of D.K. Ehrensrahl 1689. The sable and white bitch is not "Courtisane" but probably "Nespelina" (from ital. nespola, the bitch was very white). Gripsholm Castle, Sweden. (S. Tamm)

Chapter 2

AFFENPINSCHER

The Affenpinscher is believed to be of German origin. He is sometimes referred to as the Monkey dog, or Monkey Terrier and was well known on the continent of Europe as early as the 16th Century. He has been closely associated with a 15th Century Flemish painting by Jan van Eyck of Jean Arnolfini and his wife. The little shaggy terrier in the picture is generally accepted as an early Affenpinscher, although Hesketh Hubbard who wrote the chapter on The Dog in Art in Brian Vesey-Fitzgerald's *The Book of the Dog* (1948) suggests that it was a Griffon. The two breeds are similar but the Affenpinscher was accepted as being one of the breeds used in the evolution of the Griffon Bruxellois.

The dog in the painting has a slightly longer muzzle than was usual in the early 1970's but Mrs. Wendy Boorer who was very involved in the introduction of the breed to the United Kingdom tells us that a picture painted in the 19th Century by Charles Verlat shows a similar length of foreface. She suggests that this might have been usual before the necessary introduction of Griffon blood to save the Affenpinscher which came perilously close to extinction in the early part of the century. An interesting observation, which suggests that the role of the two breeds may have been reversed.

It was said in the 19th Century he was a suitable breed for ladies, although in Germany and the Low Countries he was also renowned as a keen ratter and this hunting instinct is apparent today. However, his opportunities for the sport cannot compare with the German scene in

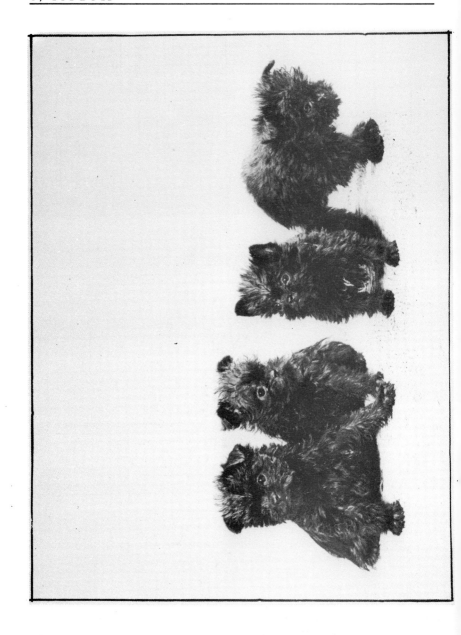

2.1 Affenpinscher. A litter of Affenpinscher puppies.
Photo: Sally Anne Thompson.

1889, when a show was organised by the German Toy Rat Terrier Club in Frankfurt and Affenpinschers were scheduled with classes for those under or over five pounds in weight.

In 1890 tribute was paid to the fanciers in Munich, particularly to Lady Şchlieber and a sheet metal worker named Ferner who owned the famous stud dog, *Zampal*. All had worked hard to establish the desired type and colour. At one time the colours were very varied and included red, wheaten, silver grey as well as the favoured colours of black, black and tan and black with grey shadings.

There was an account of the progress of the breed in this country in *Our Dogs* of 13th January 1983. Mrs. Boorer wrote that the breed had always been considered closely related to the Miniature Pinscher and she gave the following particulars:

"The Pinscher Schnauzer Klubben in 1902 listed 14 Affenpinschers as foundation stock; and in 1923 for the first time an official *standard* was published - very like today's *standard*, but still allowing a range of colours. Pedigrees given involved the names of thousands of dogs divided as follows: 600 giant schnauzers, 7,000 schnauzers, 1,500 dwarf schnauzers, 4,000 dwarf pinschers, 185 German pinschers, and 210 "monkey" pinschers."

The Affenpinscher was introduced into the United States of America during the 1930's but by 1940 the movement of livestock between Europe and America had virtually ceased due to the War. In 1936 the breed was recognised by the American Kennel Club, included in the stud book and in that year Mrs. Bessie Mally of Illinois imported *Osko von der Franziskusklause*. Another top breeder was Mrs. Henrietta Donnell, described as an internationally known toy dog expert, who bought several dogs by *Osko* from Mrs. Mally. She later showed the imported dog *Everl von der Franziskusklause* and *Nolli von Anwander*, by *Prinz von der Franziskusklause*. One of the first Affenpinschers in the United States to gain a championship was Am. Ch. *Duke of Wolf*, owned by Thelma D. Wolf.

For many more years the breed was very rare in the United Kingdom, but it had attracted the attention of Mrs. Wendy Boorer. Together with three friends Mrs. T. Teasdale, Mrs. B Hargrave and Mrs. J. Wiggins, she became sufficiently interested to import an Affenpinscher bitch, Am. Ch. *Balu's Schwarz Furstin*, from Mrs. Lucille Meystedt of Texas. Mrs. Boorer showed her in August 1975 but sadly the bitch died a year later. However, her name, *Furstin* was granted to Mrs. Boorer as her kennel affix.

Two years later Mrs. Teasdale took *Balu's Schwarz Gaba* from quarantine to Blackpool Championship Show where he won under Mr. Hamilton Renwick and later became an important stud dog. Mrs. Hargrave bred her bitch, Am. Ch. *Balu's Schwarz Leibehen* to *Gaba* and this produced one of his best sons, *Shelbor Schwarz*. A second stud dog later joined the team, German bred Int. Ch. *Deddi von Grundlachtal* but as this dog had cropped ears he was not eligible for exhibition in the United Kingdom, although he proved an excellent stud dog. Meanwhile, *Shelbor Schwarz Spinne von Champflower* was the first Affenpinscher to win a toy group and the following week his litter sister, Mrs. Wiggins's *Schwarz Spider at Scapafield* won an Open Show toy group and then best in show.

Several cropped bitches were also imported from the United States of America, and proved satisfactory brood bitches. The breed is now established in this country, thanks to the enterprise shown by the four pioneers.

These tough, hardy little dogs are fearless housedogs but not unnecessarily noisy. They make lively, devoted companions, always entertaining, sometimes described as "snub-nosed comics". An article in *Our Dogs*, 13th January, 1983, said of the breed:

"The Affenpinscher - the most fascinating, affectionate and diabolical of all Toy dogs, with the brains and the slightly mad look of its Belgian ancestors and the ambition and activity of the German breed - a lovable mixture of bravery, stubbornness, obedience and loyalty which can change in a flash from comic seriousness to utter devotion - never dull and a real friend for lonely people."

They are easy to keep in good condition. Their coats should be hard but more shaggy on the head to give the monkey-like appearance. Grooming twice a week will keep the coat in order and although they should be kept tidy they must not appear over-trimmed. Tails, undocked, are carried over the back.

The approved colour is black, although grey shading is permissable; the wide range of colour, including red, is not now recognised.

These dogs are not large, weighing from six and a half to nine pounds, and are adaptable to exercise. They are an ideal size for the house, which they prefer as they love human companionship. Like many of the toy breeds they are not very suitable as children's pets unless they are brought up with them as they are often frightened by a child's quick movements and sometimes unexpected and unintentional roughness.

2.2 Affenpinscher. Balu Schwarz Gaba.
Photo: Sally Anne Thompson.

2.3 Affenpinscher. Head Study of Balu Schwarz Gaba.
Photo: Sally Anne Thompson.

2.4 Affenpinscher Shelbor Schwarz Spinne von Champflower
Photo: Sally Anne Thompson

Chapter 3

AUSTRALIAN SILKY TERRIER

In *The Observer's Book of Dogs* (1945) Clifford L. B. Hubbard produced a photograph and gave a brief description of the Sydney Silky, saying that it first attracted some attention in the United Kingdom in 1930 when a few were exhibited. E. G. Davies in *The Book of the Dog* (1948) gave only eight lines to the breed with the additional information that it was first introduced into this country in 1928, but had made little headway. For more detail it was obviously necessary to go to the country of origin.

Mrs. Diane Banks, Publicity Officer of the Australian Silky Terrier Club says that its origin, although widely discussed, has not been definitely established. The belief is that this toy dog is the result of crossing the Australian Terrier with the Yorkshire Terrier and the slightly larger but rather similar Clydesdale Terrier, with a sprinkling of various other broken-haired Scottish-type terriers.

The Silky, according to Mrs. Banks, appeared as a breed early in this century and progressed in different parts of Australia, but the early *standards* drawn up in Victoria and New South Wales were very similar, each desiring a strong tough little dog of between six and twelve pounds in weight. The *standard* approved in 1959 by the Australian National Kennel Council, the governing body in Australia, was basically the same although more detailed, particularly in colour and size. The desirable weight was altered to between eight and ten pounds, with considerable emphasis upon soundness, terrier characteristics and gameness, at the same time not forgetting its suitability as a pet.

*3.1 An Australian Silky Terrier - Aust. Ch. Guruga Cassie Tu.
Bred by Jean Walker, owned by J.O. & Mrs. M.J. Skippen. Australia.*
Photo: Terry Dorizas

At first progeny were shown in classes for Australian Terriers or Silky Terriers, according to the breed they most resembled but in 1930 cross breeding between the Australian and Yorkshire Terriers was prohibited. From then the Silky Terrier breeders gave careful consideration to the problems which had arisen and this resulted in stabilisation of type.

On 8th December 1959 the Australian Silky Terrier Club of New South Wales was formed, and affiliated to the ANKC in the following February. At the first breed club show in September 1960 fifty-five dogs were entered. Since then the Club has grown steadily. In 1982 at the annual Battle of Champions, a prestige event organised by the Adelaide Hills Kennel Club and Harpers, the winner was a Silky, Aust. Ch. Dulcannina Laramie who had previously been the best exhibit at the Sydney Royal Show. A triumph indeed for all concerned.

Obedience titles have also been awarded in this breed, both in Australia and in the United States of America where the first Silky Terrier (the American name for the breed) was registered with the American Kennel Club in 1959 as *Winsome Beau Ideal*. Writing in *Dog World* on 2nd January 1976, Frank Warner Hill said in an article " Records are made to boast about":

"Members of the Silky Terrier Club of America are cockahoop that *Donbou Dinky of Sydney* U.D. owned by Connie and Don Alber of Springfield, Oregon, is the first toy ever to be listed with the local Sheriff's Department for Search and Rescue! This really is a first in the world for certain. Can you visualize a Silky (breed maximum weight twelve pounds) out on the line with the Sheriff's Bloodhounds? The club newsletter records that *Dinky* is the first Silky to attain the tracking title becoming a U.D.T. At the Marion County Dog Training Club tracking test on October 26th last year he was the only dog to pass and according to those in attendance only the third dog to pass a tracking test in Northern California last year.

This eight year old dog, which thoroughly enjoys his work in the First and Foremost rating, has been highest scoring toy on several occasions and missed the high in the trials by only half a point. According to his owner he will never make champion for the record books, but in her book he is all Silky and every bit a champion."

In this country interest in the breed was slow and they are the latest toy dog to achieve recognition. The first imports were late in 1974 and came from Eire. Other imports followed from Australia and Holland including two dogs *Glenpetite Wata Boy of Duskhunter* and *Yatara Dutchboy* who are behind most of the dogs now being shown. In 1978 two dogs came to England from the Dulcannina kennels in Australia.

Dulcannina Cassandra and *Dulcannina Minka*. They were bought by Mrs. J. McCoy.

The breed society was formed in 1979 and the inaugural meeting held in 1980. In seven years the total registrations increased from 7 dogs to 69 in 1985, and the breed is making good progress.

This is a well made, strong little dog, easy to keep tidy as the coat is only of medium length and although similar to a Yorkshire Terrier does not require the same amount of time spent in grooming to keep it in good condition.

We understand that, although small in size, he is healthy and agile, with the courage and tenacity of a much larger dog, adaptable and fun-loving, ideally suited as a house dog, said to be a true terrier. We have referred to his sporting instincts, but purely as a companion he is also well suited. He is said to be in demand in Australia by flat dwellers as his silky coat does not moult.

A story is told of a Silky which belonged to a family in Australia where he was the constant companion of three small children. On one occasion an intruder attempted to enter the home while the family were out. Such a storm of protest was heard that neighbours who investigated saw a man, by then anxious to get away, with the Silky firmly attached to one trouser leg. In his family and with the children, this dog had never shown the slightest aggression to anyone.

3.2 Australian Silky Terrier. Aust. Ch. Tarawera Pippin.

3.3 Australian Silky Terrier.
Head study of NZ. & Aust. Ch. Bam's Boy of Lakemba.
Photo: Michael M. Trafford.

3.4 Australian Silky Terrier. Aust. Ch. Waiton Tiny Thumbelina. From the kennels of the late Bill Maher.

Chapter 4

BICHON FRISÉ

The Bichon Frisé must be one of the oldest and most glamorous of the toy breeds. It seems incredible the first pet Bichon was only introduced into the United Kingdom three decades ago, and they were first seen in the show ring in 1973.

The small dogs of the Mediterranean were known collectively as "bichon" and it is difficult to separate their history as they were so closely connected.

The bichon Teneriffe, the Maltese, the Bolognese and the Havanese are all said to be descended from the Barbichon group. Of these the Bichon Frisé was the lap dog of the Canary Islands, hence the previous name of the bichon Teneriffe. The group is known for its intelligence - "uncommonly intelligent" Robert Leighton said of these dogs. The Maltese we deal with in a separate chapter. The Bolognese is even less known than the others, but Mrs. Jackie Ransom, an authority on these breeds, says in *The Dog Directory Guide to the bichon Frise* (1978) that its origins date back to the 11th Century. Its country of origin was of course Italy, where it was said to be held in great esteem. Mrs. Ransom relates the following story:

"The Duchess d'Este on a journey from Italy to Spain took with her as a present for his Catholic Majesty Phillip II (1527-1598) a pair of Bolognese dogs. Phillip, in a letter with his thanks, wrote 'Nothing more beautiful could be offered as a gift for a King'."

Madame de Pompadour, well known to have favoured small pet dogs, is reputed to have owned at least one Bolognese. In a Belgian book by Baron Albert Houtart published in 1925 and called *Les Epagneuls Nains Continentaux* there are two pictures of the Bolognese. One is said to have been Madame de Pompadour's dog by J. J. Bachelier (French School 1724-1806) and the other by J. A. Houdon (French School 1741- 1828) Madame de Pompadour's little dog Plon modelled in Vincennes porcelain. This has also been suggested could be a Papillon but might equally be a Bichon or perhaps a Bolognese.

Pompey was a famous Bolognese dog who featured in a book by Francis Coventry *The History of Pompey the Little* (1785) or *The Life and Adventures of a Lapdog*. He was born in Italy in 1735. He led an exciting and varied life, found himself lost in London which was the fate of many dogs in those days, and finally died at the age of fourteen years.

Mrs. Ransom thinks it likely that the Bichon was transported from the mainland by Spanish sailors to barter and sell. This theory is supported by the experience of the late Mrs. Jenkins, President of the Poodle Club, who was returning by sea from a visit to West Africa in the 1920's. The liner called at the Canary Islands where small, curly-coated white dogs were offered for sale to the passengers. These, she thought, were the Bichon Teneriffe.

The Bichon was another of the small dogs popular at the French Court, in the reign of Francis I, according to Mrs. Ransom. We have already mentioned the dogs shown in a picture of Henri III (who came to the throne 27 years later) in which a Bichon is sitting beneath his chair.

The decline in the popularity of the Bichon seems to date from 19th and early 20th centuries when they went out of fashion in their own islands. However, we understand that the Societe Centrale Canine (The French Kennel Club) approved a *standard* of points for the Bichon drawn up by the President of the Société Francais des Amateurs de chiens d'Agrément, Madam Bouctot-Vagniez, in co-operation with the Belgian authority, Madam N. Leemans. It was these authorities who suggested the more attractive name of the Bichon Frisé instead of the Bichon Teneriffe.

It is a mystery why a reasonably well known dog of such ancient origins in the continent of Europe failed to make any impact in the United Kingdom until 1973. The first Bichon seen in the show ring in this country was Mrs. Elisha Banks's *Cluneen Lejerdell Tarz Anna* imported from the United States of America who won best non- classifed at the Leeds Championship Show in May 1974. Once introduced they were hailed with enthusiasm by those looking for a glamorous show dog and pet and its rise in popularity was impressive. From the first moment the breed prospered. Registration figures rose from 354 in 1979 to 1055 in 1987.

An inaugural meeting of the Bichon Frisé Club of Great Britain was held at Caxton Hall, Westminster on 17th April 1976 and was granted recognition by the Kennel Club fifteen months later, the first Open show drawing about 78 dogs was held in January 1978. Best in show was an American import, Mrs. Wendy Streatfield's Am. Ch. *Vogelflights Choir Boy of Leander.*

The exacting scissoring necessary for the show ring in this country is unusual. The dogs in other countries are shown in a much more natural condition with only a slight tidying up, but in both the United States and the United Kingdom presentation is very important, and if kept for showing the dog is always immaculately trimmed on a regular basis. Obviously a lot of work is involved in achieving this which, to those unaccustomed to trimming, can be time consuming. Unless one is very particular the dog can be kept as a pet without this meticulous grooming and scissoring. Of course, although it will still be an attractive dog, it will not appear in quite the same perfect shape as a show dog. Bathing every two weeks and regular grooming is recommended to keep the pure white coat in good condition.

This is another breed with considerable entertainment value. In her book Mrs. Ransom says:

"Their ability to perform tricks of their own devising is quite incredible. Any ball, stick or plaything is guaranteed to bring forth a performance of amazing feats, including the toss of a ball etc. into the air followed by a complete somersault. Their knack of jumping at least three feet from a standing position, plus their habit of standing on their back legs makes it easy to understand how, for centuries, they were considered clowns and circus dogs."

Writing about temperament, she adds:

"The Bichon Frisé, small in size and a perfect companion has through the ages given pleasure to many people, from the aristocracy to the street traders and circus showring, filling each role with a charm in keeping with their present-day enchanting personality and temperament".

The accompanying pictures show this fascinating little dog in perfect show trim.

4.1 The Tresilva Bichons.
Photo: Diane Pearce

4.2 Bichon Frisé. Eng. & Ir. Ch. Tiopepi Mad Louie at Pamplona.

Chapter 5

CAVALIER KING CHARLES SPANIEL

In *The Varieties of Dogs as they are found in Old Sculptures, pictures, Engravings and Books* (1863) Ph. Charles Berjeau refers us to Israel van Meckenen, the early Dutch or German Master (1482-1498) saying that "he represented in his curious engravings" six types of dogs including spaniels and setters. Two spaniels are shown, both with average length of face, long pendant ears, fairly long in the leg and with high carried tails, one very feathered, the other less so. These must be amongst the earliest illustrations of spaniels.

Many of the Old Masters include spaniel *types*, and we think this word is significant, as it is impossible to relate most to a particular breed of spaniel. For instance, many shown in Old Dutch Masters are neither Cavalier or Papillons, as believed by many people. They are examples of the smaller Dutch red and white spaniels and in a great many cases not painted from life. None of them show the upturned face of the later King Charles spaniel.

The spaniels are a very old established group. J. H. Walsh ("Stonehenge") writing in *Dogs of the British Islands* (1867) researched the subject of spaniels which existed in the 16th Century. He stated:

"The spaniels which the upper classes fostered before the time of Charles and which had even then for many years been known and described as "toies" or toys, were (as we gather from old portraits) small, currish, white (or nearly white) little mongrels, possessing *some* spaniel character, but not much of it and almost always showing the sharp or pointed nose which marks the "cur" or mongrel. They had the spaniel ear, but not a *good* ear. They were not well feathered, and the tail frequently curled over the back. What little colour these dogs possessed was either red or liver."

It is probable that the spaniels he described were a smaller variety of the Cocker or Springer type and were the beloved toy spaniels in the 17th Century introduced into England from the continent.

However, it seems certain that the spaniels of that time were far more like the Cavalier King Charles Spaniels of today. In the early 19th Century they were superseded by the King Charles spaniels with the short, up-turned faces, who have themselves been overwhelmed in this country in recent years by the Cavalier King Charles Spaniels.

"Stonehenge" also relates interesting facts published in his book in 1867 which seems to bring nearer the times of Charles II:

"Charles II selected as his pet dog the small, large-eared short- nosed spaniel, and of course it became the favourite of the Court. The old President of Magdalen College, who died about ten years ago, in his hundredth year, was accustomed to say, that when he was a little boy he had been told by an old lady that, when she was a little girl, she saw the King walking around "Magdalen Walks" with these little dogs. The beauties of this reign were frequently painted with these pretty companions, which were succeeded by the Blenheim, or red- and-white spaniel, of equal quality and grace."

In *Stubb's Dogs* (1984) by Robert Fountain and Alfred Gates, opposite page 76, is a red and white spaniel referred to as "A brown and white King Charles in a wooded landscape". The picture was recently sold by Christies to Mr. Anthony Speelman. This beautiful painting shows a typical Cavalier with a fairly wide head, white blaze with the red spot, long nose and low carried tail. It is dated 1776 which is of course prior to the date when the head shape changed.

It may not be generally known that at the time of her accession to the throne, Queen Victoria had a favourite spaniel called *Dash*. He was tricolour, black and white with tan eyebrows. *The Ladies Kennel Journal* (1896) says:

"It was of *Dash* that the pretty story is told - we do not vouch for its accuracy, but we hope it is true - how the young Queen hurried in her royal robes, her Council of State just over, to comfort her little favourite that was lamenting her absence."

It was stated in the Journal that Her Majesty had received him as a present when she was about fiteen years old, so he had been a particular

5.1 Cavalier King Charles Spaniel.
Eng. & Aust. Ch. Amantra Captain Pugwash.
Photo: Fall

pet before she became Queen. He died on 20th December 1840 in his ninth year, according to his memorial stone in the gardens at Adelaide Lodge.

Among a number of paintings by G. Morley of the Royal dogs, is one dated 1837 of *Dash* with *Nero*, a Greyhound and *Hector*, a Deerhound.

We come now to Roswell Eldridge and his visit to London from the United States of America. He was most concerned to find the old type of King Charles Spaniel with the longer muzzle, had completely disappeared. Determined to do something about this he lost no time and at Crufts Dog Show 1926 the catalogue carried a half-page advertisement with a picture of Sir Edwin Landseer's "The Cavalier's Pets", the original of which is in the Wallace Collection, London. The catalogue heading "Blenheim Spaniels of the Old Type" continued:

"as shown in pictures of Charles II's time, long faces, no stop, flat skull, not inclined to be domed, with a spot in the centre of skull. The First Prize of £25 each in Classes 947 and 948 are given by Roswell Eldridge, Esq., of New York, and will be continued for five years. The prizes go to the nearest to type required."

In those days this was a substantial sum of money. In each case the entry was restricted to Open Dog and Open Bitch. Each class attracted two entries, and a good deal of controversy, but even four entries was a start.

A club was formed in 1928 with Miss Mostyn-Walker as chairman and Mrs. A. Pitt as honorary secretary. The first meeting was held at Crufts Dog Show that year when the breed *standard* was drawn up with Miss Mostyn-Walker's dog, *Ann's Son,* as a line pattern. This dog was born on April 27th 1927 *by Lord Pindi* ex *Ann*. He sired a bitch, *Daywell Nell,* owned by Mrs. Lawrence Brierley, *Nell* was the dam of the first Cavalier champion, *Daywell Roger,* by *Cannonhill Rickey,* who gained his title in 1948.

Mrs. Pitt, who held the *Ttiweh* prefix was untiring in her efforts to establish the Cavalier and it was largely due to her energetic leadership that the club prospered. She was subsequently chairman for over thirty years.

At Crufts Dog Show in 1929 the Cavalier King Charles Spaniel was scheduled with seven classes, excluding the two special classes sponsored by Mr. Eldridge, and the entry was 46. It is perhaps interesting to record the winners of the £25 prizes as they played a large part in the revival of the breed. These prizes continued, as promised, until 1930:

1926   Miss Mostyn-Walker's *Ann's Son* and Miss E. E. Brunne's *Hentzau Lively*.
1927   *Ann's Son* and Mrs. Raymond-Mallock's *Ashton-More Flora*.
1928   *Ann's Son* and Mrs. A. Pitt's *Hentzau Sweet Nell*.
1929   *Ann's Son* and *Ashton-More Flora*.
1930   Mrs. G. Treleaven's *Freddy of Monham* and *Ashton- More Flora*.
Unfortunately Mr. Eldridge did not live to see the successful outcome of his efforts.

In 1947 the Cavalier Club show is listed in the Kennel Club Stud Book as the only championship show for the breed that year. It was held at Stratford-on-Avon with Mrs. B Jennings as judge. The dog challenge certificate went to a grandson of *Ann's Son*, *Daywell Roger*, bred by Mrs. A. Brierley, and subsequently the first champion in the breed. Mrs. J. Eldred's *Belinda of Saxham*, at seven years old, won the bitch certificate. In those days the best of breed was not awarded. Another prize winner at the same show was *Daywell Roger's* grand-sire, *Plantation Banjo*, owned by that well known Pyrenean breeder, Madam J. Trois-Fontaines.

It has been said that other breeds were used to help in establishing the longer noses and banishing the domed heads, one being the Papillon. It seems to us important to put forward the view of an authority on the breed and we quote from *Cavalier King Charles Spaniels* (1964) in which Eilidh M. Stenning states:

"Breeders had to use 'throw-outs' from the kennels of the breeders of the flat-nosed variety - who were most co-operative and helpful. These early breeders have been accused of using other suitable breeds to get back the long noses, but this accusation was not justified, nor were the members of this small body in favour of breeding back in that way. They felt strongly that the only good way to breed back to the long noses was to do it through the long nosed 'throw-outs' but it was a hard struggle."

It is an indication of the progress of this breed that it provided the first best in show all breeds by a toy dog at Crufts Dog Show 1973. This was Ch. *Alansmere Aquarius*, a Blenheim owned by Messrs. A. Hall and J. Evans. The entry has increased tremendously since the 1920's and is now the highest in the toy group.

The Cavalier King Charles Spaniel is well known for his friendly temperament shown by his constantly wagging tail. He is usually gentle, affectionate and intelligent. These are the qualities which make him the ideal companion and family pet. Of course, as in any breed, there may sometimes be a puppy who does not possess these characteristics, but if the prospective owner deals with a reputable breeder, then naturally that possibility is reduced.

As twelve to eighteen pounds he is the largest of the toy dogs and very acceptable to men who sometimes find toy dogs an embarrassment because they are so small.

He comes in several colours. Ruby - whole coloured rich red. Blenheim - rich chestnut markings well broken up on a pearly white ground, ideally there should be a lozenge mark or spot in the centre of the white blaze. Tricolour - black and white, well spaced and broken up with tan markings over the eyes, on the cheeks, inside the ears, inside the legs and on the underside of the tail. Black and Tan - black with tan markings above the eyes, on cheeks, inside the ears, on the chest and legs and underside of the tail. Black and white is permissible but not desirable.

Occasional grooming will keep him in good condition, but if his silky coat is attended to several times a week it will be all the better for it.

*5.2 Cavalier King Charles Spaniel. Ch. Chacombe Camilla (Ruby)
and Ch. Chacombe Alexis (Tricolour).*
Photo: Fall

CH. IVAN

CH. CORDELIA

CH. CAMILLA

CH. VENETIA

CH. ZACHARY

CH. ALEXIS

5.3 Cavalier King Charles Spaniels. Owned by Mrs. D. Schilizzi.

5.4 4-month old Ruby Cavalier K.C.S. dog: McGoogans Eidolon
(Mrs. Caroline Gillies)

Chapter 6

CHIHUAHUA

This is another breed whose antecedants present a mixture of fact and fantasy. The task of separating them is very difficult. Two books, one written in 1900 and the other in 1964 give an idea of the mystery concerning this tiny breed whom journalists repeatedly assure us is the smallest dog in the world. There are two varieties, the long coat and the smooth coat and there are many different colours.

In 1900 when the breed was virtually unknown in this country, Stephen Townesend, FRCS wrote an unusual book called "*A Thoroughbred Mongrel* - the Tale of a Dog told by a Dog to lovers of dogs". Briefly it tells of a gift from Mexico:

"Today I am sending to you, under the care of my brother, who is leaving here for Europe, one of the Chihuahua dogs I promised to secure for you, if at the peril of my life. They are the smallest creatures, I believe, of the dog species Nature produces. The one I send you weighs one pound and three-quarters, and the soft-eyed Mexican from whom I bought him swore by all she held holy that he was three years old, had attained his full growth, and that age would not add one ounce to his weight. I am told that these dogs are so intelligent that they can be taught to understand any language, and so sensitive that their large eyes fill with tears at a word of reproach."

The Chihuahua arrived. The next 150 pages relate to his ups and downs, his resistance to the jealousy of less exalted dogs and to the final explanation which we will not reveal to spoil this gem of imagination.

The other book by M. Diana Russell Allen, one of the best known early Chihuahua enthusiasts in this country, is called *Little Cupid*. It is a charming fairy tale and there are beautiful illustrations. The baby Chihuahua fell out of an aeroplane and landed on the back of a goose. Fairy Beshlie, Queen of the Wings, sent a blue butterfly to care for him aided by Nell the Collie until he was reunited with his mistress:

"Back home they went to bed in the lady's bedroom on her bed and old *Nell* slept on a sofa at the foot of the bed keeping guard, and the little blue butterfly went to sleep on the petal of a beautiful white rose."

Dismissing the fairy tale, the account of the "thoroughbred mongrel" seems almost credible and is proof that the Chihuahua was known in the United Kingdom early in this century, although not officially recognised until many years later. Miss Rosina Caselli, said in *Our Dogs* of 6th August 1904:

"Chihuahuas were in their natural state, a distinctly Mexican race of wild dogs, and for their size very savage."

She added that in Mexico they inhabited a limited part of the mountainous state of Chihuahua and had been seen by natives 'up to about fifteen years ago'. She thought that some might still be found in 'undisturbed' places. She suggested that these dogs were plentiful until the Mexican Central Railroad was opened about 1887, when the nature of the country altered, and the dogs were scattered in all directions. Her account is convincing, but there seems to be no reply to the views of Dr. Isad Ochoterene, one of the greatest paleontologists in Latin America, who said:

"No dog fossils have ever been discovered in Mexico, either in graves or other parts. I declare that I am totally ignorant as to the origin of the story of the Chihuahua dog being a native of Chihuahua, and furthermore that it can be found wild in that state."

It could be hoped that historical research might provide some evidence such as the experience of explorers or other people whose occupations involved them in travelling throughout the country. Some followers of Columbus thought they may have seen small dogs, but never stated categorically they were dogs, saying they looked like dogs, or could have been dogs. Others suggested they could equally have been an animal called the Perro Chihuahueno, possibly an early ancestor of the Chihuahua, or even the Techichi, said to be a species of rodent which bore some slight resemblance to a dog and of which there were many varieties in Mexico. However, this animal was described by Lieut. Colonel Chas. Hamilton-Smith, writing in Sir William Jardine's *Naturalists Library* 1839/1840, as follows:

"We have seen only one individual of this race, by the Indians called Techichi. It was a long backed heavy looking animal, with a terrier's mouth, tail and colour; but the hair was scantier and smoother, and the ears were cropped. It is likely that the specimen seen by us at Rio de San Juan was of the same race as the Techichi described by Fernandez."

Mrs. Hilary Harmar, writing in *Chihuahuas* (1966) describes her experiences when she and her husband joined an archeological expedition at Teotihuacan. This is quite close to Acolman where dog markets were held and about 400 dogs offered for sale daily. She had hoped to find evidence of the Chihuahua, but there was no sign of a dog skeleton. In the same book Mrs. Harmar says the breed was known in Malta, Sardinia and Venice for centuries and suggests they might have been brought to Mexico by the Conquistadores after the wars with Spain. It would seem more likely that dogs were taken from country to country by traders than by a conquering army. In support of the theory that the breed had been known in Europe is a painting by Botticelli in 1481/2. There is no doubt that the little dog in the Sistine Chapel Fresco "The Sons of Moses" is of the Chihuahua type. Mrs. Harmar suggests that Bull Terrier fanciers "might claim it" but to us its size perspective, details of the head and particularly the fine feet with long claws make it unmistakably a small Chihuahua- type dog.

The early history of the breed cannot be more than speculation. Numerous theories have been discussed in several books. Although the original home of the Chihuahua is in considerable doubt we can be sure of later statements made at the end of the 19th Century. Writing in *Country Life in America*, a magazine published in March 1914, James Watson relates the following interesting story:

"Upon the occasion of Madam Adaline Patti's farewell appearance in Mexico, the then President of the Republic, General Portferio Diaz, honored her with a reception and presented her with a magnificent bouquet of flowers. Hidden among the blossoms (as if one of them) the great diva found a tiny Chihuahua dog. Of course, in consideration of both the donor and the recipient, the specimen was a magnificent one and, despite its minute size, thoroughly sound. Mme. Patti adopted the animal at once, named it *Bonito*, and carried it with her wherever she went all over the world. *Bonito* lived for a long span of years and after his death Mme. Patti obtained other Chihuahuas. This was before the time that Chihuahuas were well known outside Mexico, and the dogs of the great singer were a sensation wherever she went."

This story was quoted in *The Complete Chihuahua* (1967) which was written by seven experts on the breed for Howell Book House Inc. of New York.

In the last part of the 19th Century it was common for Mexicans living on the border with the United States to follow a lucrative trade by offering tourists tiny, often unsound, dogs. James Watson relates his experience when returning from a judging trip in Mexico in 1888:

"Had it not been that we had no Pomeranians in the country at that time I should have said she was of that kin. Her coat was like Beaver fur both as to color and texture, and she was so small that I carried her in my pocket till I got to Los Angeles, and there got the smallest chip basket in which she had plenty of room."

The first Chihuahua registered with the American Kennel Club was called *Midget* in 1904. The first to be shown in the United States was *Chi Chigas* entered as a Chihuahua Terrier in the class for Miscellaneous and Foreign Dogs at the Philadelphia Kennel Club, 17th - 19th September 1884 and the first to become a champion was *Beppie*, a fawn and white, the property of Mrs. L. A. McLean of New Jersey.

The Chihuahua Club of America was formed in 1923 and the well known strains responsible for many of our good English lines were established. Mr. Russell E. Kauffman mentions a long-coat Chihuahua named *Caranza*:

"He was about 2 1/2 to 3 pounds of a dark fiery red, his tail like that of a squirrel. His head was perfect by the *standard* we have today. His eyes were ruby red, ears fringed not unlike that of the Papillon."

As this dog was born early in this century it establishes the fact that a long coat was known in the United States in the very early days, although it was said that he could not have been pure bred as Chihuahuas were always smooth coated. This dog founded two of the best known American lines - *Perrito* and *Meron*.

Although Robert Leighton mentions the Chihuahua in *The New Book of the Dog* (1912) and shows a photograph of a Mexican imported dog, the breed was hardly known in this country until shortly before the Second World War when one of the first breeders, Mrs. W. S. Powell, imported some dogs from Mexico in 1935, but sadly her home in Clapham Common, London, received a direct hit during an air raid, killing her dogs and leaving her a hopeless invalid.

This fascinating breed is very popular. It has an unusual flat tail, a special feature, and both varieties make excellent pets, particularly for those who favour the less independent type. They are gay, alert, quick of

6.1 Chihuahua. Ch. Yeosinga Spellbinder (Longcoat) as a puppy.
Photo: Diane Pearce

hearing and good house dogs. Many do not care for strangers, but they are very affectionate towards their owners and demand a lot of attention in return. Generally they are sweet tempered and not easily upset, although many are afraid of children. Most like to be covered during the night, preferably on their owner's bed, and if they can wheedle their way under the covers they consider this ideal. They are no problem to groom and inexpensive to feed. At the present time the Longcoat tends to be the more popular but the smooth variety is a smart little dog.

In January 1961 the Kennel Club separated the two varieties for show purposes. Recently they have divided the breed into two distinct varieties according to the coat - the Longcoat and the Smoothcoat.

The breed *standard* gives a weight from two pounds to six pounds, but adds that the preferred weight is two pounds to four pounds, saying that if two dogs are equally good in type the more diminutive is preferred. We would point out that as a pet it is preferable to choose the larger dog which should have more stamina and may be sounder in body and limb. A dog of the minimum weight given demands a great deal of care and consideration.

An interesting point which perhaps emphasises the versatility of these small dogs is their use in show business by two breed personalities. One we have already mentioned is Miss Rosina Caselli who owned a troupe of Chihuahuas at the beginning of this century and toured the music halls. In the 1960's one of our leading Chihuahua authorities, Mrs. Olga Frei-Denver, the first secretary of the Longcoat Chihuahua Club, trained a group of these intelligent little dogs which became well known professionally in this country. Individually they can sometimes be seen at the present time in films and on the stage.

6.2 Chihuahua. Ch. Anyako Benjamin (Longcoat).
Photo: Marc Henrie, ASC.

6.3 Chihuahua. Ch. Anyako Amazing Grace (Smoothcoat).
Photo: Marc Henrie, ASC.

Chapter 7

CHINESE CRESTED DOG

Hilary Harmar, in *The Complete Chihuahua Encyclopaedia* (1972) suggests it is just possible the Mexican hairless dogs arrived in Mexico from China between the fourth and seventh centuries B.C. during the late Chou dynasty. She also suggests they may have arrived during the 18th Century when a Chinese ship called annually at Acapulco. She says:

"These dogs are often called 'China Pelona' meaning 'Chinese Hairless'."

In the 1st edition of *Dogs of the British Islands* (1867) "Stonehenge" refers to the fact that the Chinese Edible Dog had been well known in this country as a curiosity but it is unusual to find a mention of the Chinese Crested at such an early date. An engraving depicts a year old bitch, who came from a litter of six, the others and the parents having died.

Rawdon B. Lee in *A History and Description of Modern Dogs* (1899) quotes W. K. Taunton, a noted judge of the time and owner of a Chinese Crested:

"In China are found several different breeds of dogs, many of which bear a very close resemblance and are probably identical with some of the breeds of other countries. As an instance, there can be little doubt the hairless dog of China is the same as the Mexican hairless dog, and the crested dogs bear a striking resemblance to the dogs which have lately been exhibited and described as African Sand dogs...."

7.1 Chinese Crested Dog. Ch. Petworth Moppy Top.
Photo: David J. Lindsay.

7.2 Chinese Crested Dog. Kojak Kavalkade.
Photo: Diane Pearce

A well known writer and leading judge of dogs, Charles H. Lane, in *All About Dogs* (1900) referred to the Chinese Crested as one of the outlandish breeds of which he had seen very few specimens. He went on to state:

"From what I have seen of them, I should consider them delicate, and unsuited for our climate, except under favourable circumstances."

This is the inference one would draw, but the Crested is tough and the English winter appears to hold no terrors for him. It is the very hot weather which is sometimes inclined to distress him unless his skin is cared for and oiled to prevent cracking.

Mr. Lane included an engraving by R. H. Moore, one of the chief dog artists at that time, of W. K. Taunton's *Chinese Emperor*.

C. L. B. Hubbard, in *The Observer's book of Dogs* (1945) stated the hairless dogs of Africa, China and Mexico were closely allied and points out that the Chinese Crested dog only differed from the others by means of a tuft of long hairs on the skull and tail. He continued:

"The race is practically extinct in China, and the so-called Chinese Crested dogs exhibited at various peep-shows are quite dissimilar from the breed described in the reference books of China some 400 years ago."

In *Hutchinsons Illustrated Dog Encyclopaedia* (1935) the breed is classed with the African Sand dog but referred to as the Chinese Hairless.

Ada Milner in *Les Chiens d'Agrement* (1924) devoted only a few lines to Hairless dogs and there are two small photographs of dogs she refers to as Mexican which she states were known in London in 1897. One of the dogs appears to be a Chinese Crested dog *Paderewski Junior* owned by Mr. H C Brooke.

Another famous winner owned by Mr. Brooke was *Hairy King* and these two were usually shown in books which mentioned the breed. They were said to be exceedingly intelligent and keen to hunt rats and rabbits.

The hairless dog is not unique. Count de Bylandt in *Dogs of All Nations* (1905) said:

"...their origin is very different, Central and South America, Patagonia, South Africa, Mexico and China, all have their hairless dogs..."

However, the Chinese Crested is unique, as it is the only known breed to produce a hairless and a full coated dog in the same litter. Other hairless breeds have a counterpart which is smooth coated but never a long coated one as seen in the photograph on page 41.

This extraordinary phenomenon cannot be bred out, the two types are anatomically identical, and to attempt to do so would seriously harm the breed. It is strange that no mention has been made in the early books of this curious fact, but it might be explained because the breed was not taken very seriously in the early days. However, there have been references to puppy mortality and this may have been a cause.

In recent times the breed has attracted more attention in the United Kingdom and at first an attempt was made to breed out the full coated type known as Powderpuff. This was soon found to be genetically impossible. The position was accepted and the two types now compete in the show ring on equal terms. A further complication is that each type has its own variations. The Powderpuff variety either has a long veil coat and dropped ears or a short veil and perhaps prick ears. The hairless variety can have a long profuse crest, similar to that of a pony's mane, or just a small crest. Both the hairless varieties have plumed tails and usually "socks".

The skin of the hairless is smooth and warm to the touch, usually a slatey-grey, or grey and white, or a deep shade of pink and blue-grey, known as lace. It is popularly believed that the temperature of the hairless Chinese Crested dog is slightly higher than the normal reading of 101.5 (38.7c), but, strange to say, this is a moot point. In Mirri Cardew's *A Chinese Crested for me* (1986) we are told:

"... most Hairless have a normal temperature of 103 F (39.4c). The Powderpuffs seem to be the normal 101.4 (38.7c).

Some breeders agree with Mrs. Cardew although there does not appear to be any scientific evidence to substantiate this view.

The Powderpuffs have an undercoat with a soft veil of long hair and there are various colours. One seen at Crufts Dog Show 1986 was a glamorous cream colour.

At the Birmingham City Championship Show 1986, the first Powderpuff to become a champion in the breed was Mrs. M Godfrey's *The Master Blaster of Pekiki,*, by *Heathermount Victor* ex *Cartergate Anna.*

Both the hairness and the coated variety can occur in the same litter. The hairless feature is dominant. If two hairless dogs are bred together there can be a small proportion of coated puppies. Two powderpuffs will produce only Powderpuffs, whilst breeding a hairless and a Powderpuff together one might expect half of each type. In the hairless dogs the dentition has been a problem. Often the dog is born with missing teeth, or, through lack of the correct amount of enamel on the teeth, they are lost very early in life. Through careful mating, paying attention to this problem, the position is improving. The Powderpuffs have, as a rule, perfect mouths with strong jaws and bite.

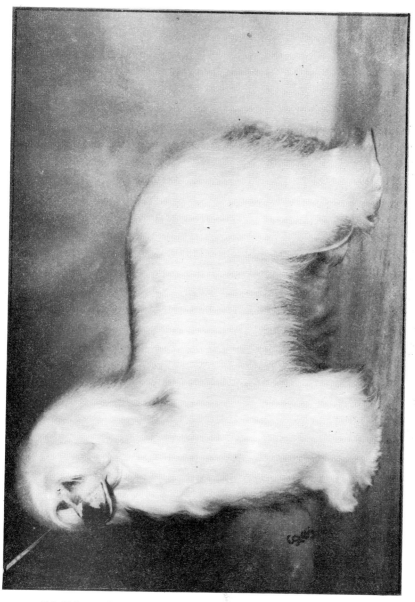

7.3 Chinese Crested Dog. Colboxhall Hellmutt. (Powderpuff).
Photo: Russell Fine Art

These facts are usually of little consequence to the owner of a pet, but if breeding is contemplated it is advisable to discuss with the breeder this particular genetic peculiarity before buying the foundation bitch. Trying to tamper with this condition with the object of breeding only hairless could have a harmful effect upon the breed generally.

Obviously grooming the hairless dogs is not a problem. To keep the skin in good condition it is essential to watch it carefully and to oil at regular intervals, particularly in hot weather. It is important to use a good quality oil such as Oil of Ulay, or a mixture of glycerine and rosewater. The feet are hare shaped and feathered, the claws of moderate length similar to a Chihuahua foot. Powderpuffs should be groomed regularly, daily if possible.

For those seeking an unusual breed this exotic looking graceful little dog is certainly something different. It is doubtful if he will ever be a commercial proposition - to many pet owners this is an asset. In their own homes or among friends they are highly intelligent, sweet and affectionate pets, obedient and good housedogs, not immediately sociable with strangers. Although they are not nervous they are reticent to make friends unless given time.

They are also a tough breed with hunting instincts. They will not as a rule harm animals in their own household and will live in harmony with them, but they are always keen to go rabbiting. They move swiftly and are good ratters. Unless stopped as puppies they may chase birds and given the opportunity will eagerly pursue deer.

They are not so suitable as pets for children unless brought up with them as one of the family.

It has been suggested that this breed can be acceptable for anyone allergic to dog hairs.

Chapter 8

CLYDESDALE TERRIER

Unfortunately it is common to hear of many breeds of farm animals particularly chickens and bantams, which have become almost, or completely, extinct. Probably the only toy breed of note to which this has happened is the Clydesdale Terrier.

This dog, a native of the Clyde Valley was also known as the Paisley Terrier. He was one of the larger toy breeds weighing up to sixteen pounds. At first sight there is a remarkable similarity to the Skye Terrier, but in fact he differed materially from this larger dog.

He was very handsome and a feature was his long, straight silky coat, without undercoat, hanging straight down each side from a centre parting. From neck to tail he was a bright steel blue colour, head, legs and feet of golden tan. His ears small and set very high, covered with long silky hair and carried pricked. His tail was very dark blue or black and heavily feathered. The texture and colour of the coat was very important and the scale of points, a favourite form of assessment at the beginning of the century, gave 50 out of a total of 100 points to these two features alone.

We understand that it was not easy to produce the perfect type and, like the Skye and Yorkshire Terriers, difficult to maintain the coat in top show condition. Some breeders kept their dogs in grease, customary today for the show Yorkshire Terrier, and daily grooming could never be neglected. They were pretty dogs but according to the sporting gentlemen of the period were "useless lady's pets", but this was said of

8.1 Clydesdale Terrier. An extinct Toy breed sometimes known as the Paisley Terrier and thought to be an antecedent of the Yorkshire Terrier.

most lap-dogs. However, they were said to be "good at vermin" a redeeming feature in those times, and useful little house dogs.

One of the leading breeders was Sir Claud Alexander, a great animal lover whose home at Faygate Wood, Sussex, housed a fine collection of all types of wild animals in addition to his kennels of Skye and Clydesdale Terriers, Rough and Smooth Collies, and other breeds of dog. He was also reputed to have a fine cattery. Among his champion Clydesdale Terriers was *Ballochmyle Wee Wattie*, whose photograph has often been used in old books to illustrate a typical specimen of the breed. Another well known breeder was Mr. Thomas Erskine who showed *Lorne of Donne* and his son, ex *Blythewood Pearl*, a great winner and we are told "a picture to look at".

Many consider the Clydesdale almost certainly played a large part in the development of the Yorkshire Terrier, a breed which he closely resembled except for size.

A breed club was formed for the Clydesdale Terrier in 1884 but unfortunately residents of the valley favoured the name of Paisley Terrier. According to Mr. Rawdon B. Lee another club was formed under that name which withheld all support from the Clydesdale Terrier Club and neither was registered with the Kennel Club. By the time it was realised how seriously this split was affecting an already numerically small breed the harm was done and it was too late to revive interest.

The breed had a reputation for good temperament, also being affectionate, intelligent and alert. What a pity the Clydesdale, with so many good qualities and indigenous to the United Kingdom never achieved sufficient popularity to ensure his survival. It was said that many of the principal fanciers were weavers and their dogs accompanied them to work. When machines began to replace hand looms this custom had to be stopped and no doubt this also contributed to waning interest.

Although saved from extinction in 1936 this did not endure and the breed has rarely been seen or heard of since that time.

8.2   *Clydesdale Terrier. Mr. G. Shaw's Mozart.*
(The New Book of the Dog, Robert Leighton)

Chapter 9

ENGLISH TOY TERRIER (BLACK AND TAN)

It is surprising that so little has been written about toy breeds which are indigenous to this country and of these breeds the English Toy Terrier must be one of the least documented, as apart form several works of fiction there are very few monographs on this breed.

To avoid confusion perhaps we should mention at this point that the larger type was first known as the Black and Tan Terrier, later as the Manchester Terrier. The small dogs were called the Toy Terrier (smooth); renamed as the Black and Tan Terrier (Miniature) and latterly as the English Toy Terrier. Some early writers referred to the breed as the English Terrier (Black and Tan).

C. H. Lane in *Dog Shows and Doggy People* (1902) remembered the time when the breed was shown in "large, medium and small" divisions and commanded some of the biggest entries amongst the non- sporting section "at our best shows". Except for size, the breed *standard* was exactly the same for black and tans with weight variation between seven and twenty-five pounds.

In *The Terrier* magazine of January 1948 a well known breeder and exhibitor Mrs. Eleanor Dann, believed that the Miniature Black and Tan Terrier was first seen in 1870, bred by a veterinary surgeon in Bury, Lancashire. This implies that the popularity of the small type was quickly established, although the size range was quite large, which makes it difficult to say exactly when the breed became a "toy dog".

It was of course usual in those days for the few registered toy breeds to be considered just ladies pets and the following extract by Hugh Dalziel in "Stonehenge's (J. H. Walsh) *Dogs of the British Islands* (1878) illustrates this point:

"I am writing of the dog from 10 lbs. to 16 lbs. not the small lap dogs of the same colour and markings, which are generally pampered and peevish, and ornamental rather than useful - which, when they do give tongue at the entrance of a visitor, never know when they have yelped enough, and have to be coaxed into silence. These latter are of two sorts; one with a short face, round skull, and full eye (inclined to weep), called in vulgar parlance "apple-headed 'uns" showing the cross at some time or other with the King Charles spaniel; the other type is a shivering dog, that must be kept clothed, and sleep in a warmly lined basket, his timid shrinking manner, spindly legs, lean sides and tucked-up flanks showing the Italian Greyhound cross. The weight of these two clearly distinct varieties averages from about 3 lbs to 6 lbs."

"Stonehenge", doubtless feeling that further comment was desirable, said of the breed:

"Such is no doubt, a fair description of the ordinary toy terrier but there is a third variety represented by *Belle*, which, although extremely rare, still exists in considerable numbers. This little dog is, in fact, the large black and tan terrier reduced in size from 15 lbs. or 16 lbs. to 3 lbs. or 4 lbs. and possessed of equal hardihood and spirit ...the great difficulty is to breed such little dwarfs without loss of symmetry or substance, the general result being a reduction of the size of the body and an enlargement proportionately of the head."

In the 1st edition of Mr. Dalziel's own publication, *British Dogs*, 1879-1880, he wrote of the Black and Tan Toy Terrier under his nom-de-plume of "Corsincon", in a much less disdainful manner and appeared to subscribe to the views of "Stonehenge". He even recommended an ointment to encourage the better growth of coat, a difficulty which was connected with the necessary close breeding to reduce size.

The terrier, *Belle*, mentioned by "Stonehenge" was one of the noted winners of that time. She was owned by Mr. Howard Maplebeck but her pedigree was unknown.

A fair description of the Black and Tan was given in *The Twentieth Century Dog* (1904). Mr. T W Tweed, said to have been "an old professional fancier" stated that, although he was well aware of the desirable type in this breed, the demand was for an apple-headed type as all the ladies asked for small dogs with short faces:

9.1 English Toy Terrier (Black & Tan). Head Study of Ch. Scarteen Sea Wyf.
Photo: Diane Pearce.

9.2 English Toy Terrier (Black & Tan). Ch. Scarteen Sea Wyf.
Photo: Diane Pearce.

"My own idea of a perfect toy is a dog with a black nose, level teeth and not pig-faced; long, level head; small dark eyes; erect ears, not too big; well filled up under the eyes - in fact, wedge- shaped head; arched neck, legs as near fox-terrier's as possible; deep chest; short, compact body; tail short and thin, and carried as low as possible; colour of tan, rich mahogany, with the correct markings, and the spots on the cheeks as far apart as possible. But the type I find the most saleable is different. There you want short face; small, erect ears, short back and tail, and rather more tan than ordinary. The weight, at a year old, should vary from 3 to 5 lbs. They must have *pretty* faces, or they do not fetch much."

There was a divergence of opinion about the popularity of these dogs. In 1907 Theo. Marples thought that the toy black and tan terrier, which he called a sub-variety of the larger dog, was probably more numerous and popular than his prototype. He noted that the smaller ones were probably more valuable but stressed the necessity for length and leanness of head and symmetry, points also mentioned by C. L. B. Hubbard in the much later 1st edition of *The Observer's Book of Dogs* (1945).

"Here is quite an old English product of the Toy Breed Fancy and one widely known but not great in numbers. It is a diminutive Manchester Terrier, almost exactly, for its shape, colour and coat are practically identical with those of its parent type. In the 1870"s the Miniature Black and Tan Terrier was very popular in London, where the fashionable weight for these dogs never exceeded 7 lbs .... a common fault at that time, however, was to sacrifice for lack of size the more important soundness and symmetry which is as essential to this little dog as to any larger animal."

In the *Complete Toy Manchester Terrier* (1950) published in the United States of America, Dixie Dempsey states that the breed was well known in the 1890's and she remembered her aunt possessed one. They were common around farms and chicken houses and probably used to keep down the rat population. They were about seven to nine pounds in weight. Mrs. Dempsey says:

"My mother-in-law told stories of the little black and tan dogs in her childhood home in Pennsylvania that were known as "creepers" .... residents of the vicinity used them as hunting dogs, mostly in fox hunting through the dense thickets. They were used on squirrels too, and are said to have been able to climb trees after their game... One particular dog ran with the Coon hounds. In Louisiana, the black and tan squirrel dog has been bred for generations. No-one knows when or from where the

Illustrations du Journal "L'ACCLIMATATION" 46, Rue du Bac, Paris

Race TOY TERRIER
Chiens minuscules pesant de 2 à 3 kilos.

9.3 English Toy Terrier (Black & Tan). An early postcard.

9.4 English Toy Terrier (Black & Tan). Christmas card of the English Toy Terrier Club.

first of these appeared there, but all are distinctly Manchester, even though a trifle heavier in body than today's show type."

In the *American Kennel Club Stud Book* for 1886 under "Toy Terriers other than Yorkshires" is listed a Black and Tan named *Gypsy*, number 4485, owned by L. F. Whitman of Chicago which Mrs. Dempsey says was officially the first American Toy Manchester Terrier. However, as the List of Registered Breeds given in *The AKC's World of the Pure-Bred Dog* (1985) gives this name and number to a Manchester Terrier in the Terrier section and makes no mention of it under Toy Breeds, its accuracy cannot be guaranteed.

For another forty years in the United States the breed came under "Toy Terriers other than Yorkshires". Then a special plea was made by Mrs. Lillian C. Raymond Mallock, a toy dog enthusiast, formerly Miss L. C. Moeran, resident in America before her marriage and later known to us as the breeder of the Ashton More Pekingese and King Charles Spaniels. She feared the extinction of the Black and Tans as their decline in popularity was significant, probably due to the insistence upon very tiny dogs, some weighing as little as three or four pounds. She thought that separate classification might further their interests, and in 1926 the Toy Black and Tan Terrier was officially recognised. The breed was known by that name until 1934, when the American Kennel Club changed the classification and this little dog became the Toy Manchester Terrier, as it is called in America today. The breed is now more popular in the United States than this country.

Mrs. Dann described the breed as alert, sturdy, easy to feed and extremely lovable and faithful. Grooming will keep the coat in good condition and it is advisable to brush the dog daily with a medium bristle brush to keep it free from dirt and dust. She suggests an occasional application of olive oil, followed by a rub with a chamois leather. If desired, the coat can be "polished" with a silk scarf or handkerchief which will give it a shine and make a great difference to the dog's appearance. If he is attended to regularly he will seldom need a bath, but if he is bathed make sure he is perfectly dry before he is allowed out, particularly in winter time.

In these days when the criteria of a breed has changed and a toy terrier is appreciated as a pet rather than a killer of vermin, the English Toy Terrier deserves more popularity. He has not lost his gameness and sporting instincts or his ability to defend himself if provoked, but as a house dog he is ideal. He is small and neat, takes little room and makes sure his warnings are heard. He is devoted to his owner, gay and ever ready for a good walk. It must be remembered that he cannot tolerate very cold weather. The wise owner will provide a coat if the weather is particularly bad and will take care not to shut him out in the garden for longer than necessary. A short brisk walk in winter time is preferable to standing about in the garden for any length of time.

For those interested in books about their breed we must mention particularly one book which gave the breed some publicity when published in about 1915, called *Terrier V.C.* by Julia Lowndes Tracy, with a "Note" by Lady Smith-Dorrien. Proceeds from sales were donated to the Blue Cross Fund, which was responsible then for good work in France among horses. It is dedicated to *Star*, who followed his master to France, and received the same decoration in miniature as that awarded to his master by King George V. This anecdote is said to be true. The illustrations are by that famous artist who devoted so much time to the cat - Louis Wain. Other books are listed in the Bibliography.

9.5 A group of Toy Terriers.

9.6 English Toy Terrier. Late 19th Century Manchester Terrier and Toy, showing the contrast in size.

Chapter 10

GRIFFON BRUXELLOIS

The Griffon Bruxellois is certainly of Belgian origin and we consider it rightly claimed in the booklet published by the Société Royale Saint-Hubert (the Belgian Kennel Club) which gives the *standards* of native breeds. The evidence of this is conclusive. However, doubts have been expressed by certain authorities. Mr. Rawdon B. Lee maintained that the Griffon originated in Great Britain and was a cross between the Irish and Yorkshire Terriers, so we understand from L. G. (Doone) Raynham in *The History and Management of the Griffon Bruxellois* (1985). The grounds for Mr. Lee's supposition are slender. On the other hand an American, Mr. James Watson, in his two volume work *The Dog Book* (1906) suggested a relationship with an old Dutch breed and said that if Belgian breeders would turn to the Hollandsche Smoushond they would not fail to find the dog from which the Griffon Bruxellois was sported as a lady's pet. He said:

"Belgian fanciers let nature take its course in the matter of skull in their miniature Smoushond."

A clear example of a Griffon type of dog is shown in Jan van Eyck's painting of The Marriage of Jean Arnolfini and Giovanna Cenami (1434) in the National Gallery, London, which shows an obvious resemblance between the Affenpinscher and the Griffon, said to be descended from the Affenpinscher.

In her book *Toy Dogs and How to Breed and Rear Them* (1902) Mrs. M. Handley Spicer states:

"My own opinion is that the Griffon Bruxellois is a modified and improved edition of the Affenpinscher."

Mrs. Handley Spicer's book deals almost exclusively with the management and care of the Griffon and this is her only observation on origins.

Mr. Will Hally, who enjoyed a reputation as an authority on "foreign dogs" during the first half of this century, stated that he disagreed emphatically with Mr. Lee's statement that Irish and Yorkshire Terriers were in any way concerned with the background of the Griffon. He thought that the German Miniature Pinscher had probably been used and could account for some of the terrier characteristics in the breed. He stated:

"Quite glaringly, the Griffon is very closely related to the little Affenpinschers which a few of us youthful enthusiasts used to import from Germany in the days before the quarantine laws .. The early importations of Griffons show Affenpinscher and Toy Spaniel parentage very decidedly."

A certain amount of later history of the breed in Belgium is known. Like many of the other toy breeds, it was popular at the Court. Edward C. Ash says:

"Queen Marie of Belgium was keenly interested in the breed and when she died a dog called *Whin* was left in the care of a servant together with a legacy of £2,000 to be looked after and have all it needed for the rest of its life."

Griffons were also known as the small, rough ratting dogs of the hackney coachmen, bred in the more lowly conditions of the stable. Ratting was indicative of the terrier-like instincts found in the Affenpinscher.

A well known Belgian breeder, Madam Warzée of the Chenil du Clos des Orchidées prefix was instrumental in reviving the breed after the second World War. In *Griffon Bruxellois* (1960) Miss M. Cousens quotes a letter from her describing a type of dog, semi-Barbet, semi- Griffon, of the 1880's:

"The muzzle was pointed, elongated, the coat less wiry, the tuft on the head silky. It was multi-coloured, with sometimes white on the head and legs."

Madame Warzée believed that the Yorkshire Terrier was involved in the development of the Griffon and one of the salient points was a silky topknot which was common in the old type Griffon. She tells of a dog of the type described which was best in show on the Field of Manoeuvres

10.1 Griffon Bruxellois. Ch. Starbeck Crystal Rainbow.
Photo: Fall

10.2 Griffon Bruxellois (Petit Brabancon - smooth coated).
Ch. Speedwell Suzy.
Photo: Diane Pearce.

near Brussels, in the 1880's, which was bought and exported to the United Kingdom by Mr. Marchison. This encouraged Belgian breeders to try to obtain more like it. Miss Cousens mentions in her book a theory of her own:

"That there always has existed a breed of small rough-haired dogs, as early as the fifteenth century or before, and that those were the forerunners of the Affenpinscher. And that it was the Affenpinscher which was being kept in the back streets of Brussels in the mid-nineteenth century, from which sprang the winner of 1880, and which, crossed later with the various other breeds mentioned, eventually produced the Griffon Bruxellois."

One of the pioneers said by Miss Cousens to have done more for the breed than anyone else in its history, was Mrs. Handley Spicer of the *Copthorne* prefix who produced many champions and was largely instrumental in the formation of the Griffon Club. Her husband, later Sir Howard Handley Spicer, was a lover of animals all his life, a member of the Kennel Club, an authority on Griffons and particularly interested in all the toy breeds. Mrs. Handley Spicer wrote a long article after a club show at the Royal Horticultural Hall, Westminster on 11th April 1907. Lack of space prevents a full account but the following observations are of particular interest:

"Having been present at practically every Griffon show of importance either in this country or abroad for the last ten years I can safely say that this one was far and away the finest I have ever attended both as regards the number and quality of the exhibits. It was indeed a magnificent show. Ten years ago the Brussels Griffon was, to a great extent, a breed looked down upon, one which was barely established in points, one which failed to breed true to type, and one in which all the good specimens in existence could easily be counted on one's fingers. Today, as the Westminster show amply demonstrated, all that is changed.

The English, as a nation, have natural aptitude for improving and developing the quality of livestock, and having adopted the Brussels Griffon as our own, we see the breed rapidly and steadily improving both in appearance and popularity, whilst those of us who have for years been striving to improve the breed, have now the joy and satisfaction of seeing the Griffon of our dreams, typical, alert, full of expression and quality springing up on every hand."

It was only three years previously that Mrs. J H Whaley, an early breeder wrote in *The Twentieth Century Dog* (1904):

"The type, as it exists, is too varied. Not enough importance is attached to colour, eyes, carriage of ears, and the dogs being well undershot. These points should be clearly defined for the benefit of breeders."

At that time there was still some divergence of type, but the position had obviously improved by 1910 when Toy Notes in the *Illustrated Kennel News* stated:

"Quite a good entry of Griffons were benched for Miss Newill's judgement at the LKA Members Show, a class of twelve being quite exceptional... What a spurt this breed has made lately as all the records show! At Fulham and the LKA Members Shows the quality was specially noticeable, and the numbers most encouraging... We are looking forward with confidence to the Griffon, quaint little beast as he is, and full of tricky ways - becoming one of the most popular of the toy breeds. It is pleasing to note the great improvement that has been made in under-jaws, expression and texture of coat, and now that these points are being understood and bred for, a greater uniformity of type may be expected."

The Griffon Bruxellois Club was accepted for registration by the Kennel Club on 11th October 1898. Miss Adela Gordon, the first secretary applied for classification on the register of breeds on 13th April 1898, but a full statement signed by members of the club was required, so acceptance was not finally granted until 7th March 1899. In the Kennel Club Stud Book for that year breed details left the columns of "Foreign Dogs" and took their place under the Griffon Bruxellois. The first British bred winner was a dog called *Sapristi*, sired by *Porthos*, one of the first Belgian imports.

Mrs. Handley Spicer referred to two breed clubs, saying that in the Autumn of 1902 another club had been formed to promote the breed and she considered it the more useful and important of the two. She added that her pride was only natural as she had the honour to be an active member. This second club was accepted for registration by the Kennel Club on 4th February 1902 as the Bruxellois Griffon Club of London, but its name was subsequently changed to the Brussels Griffon Club of London. Although it started well it did not prosper and collapsed after a short time.

There are two varieties of the breed. The smooth coated, called the Petit Brabancon which is a very attractive little dog and widely popular in Belgium. They were said to be one of the chief attractions at a show in Edinburgh in October 1904. The smooth, glossy coat presents no problems if it is kept brushed regularly. The rough coated type has a harsh double coat and in addition to regular grooming the coat has to be stripped, preferably by hand. Clipping does not remove the dead undercoat, but merely cuts the coat and sometimes can affect the colour. Only on the stomach is the coat removed by clippers. It is advisable and much easier to have the coat attended to professionally twice a year. The photographs show the difference in appearance of the two types.

The Griffon has a terrier-like temperament and sporting instincts, to be expected when one reads of his ancestry. Although small, he is very determined almost to the point of being stubborn, but full of character. He is certainly not subservient and, as a well known owner has observed, fawning dependence can never be achieved in this breed.

He is sensitive however and needs gentle handling. Puppies are often slightly apprehensive of anything new which they do not understand, but the quick intelligence of the breed will soon restore their habitual bold and lively approach.

In the past one often heard the rough Griffon described as "quasi-human"; an apt term, no doubt partly on account of his beard. The breed *standard* now describes him as monkey-like. The fact remains that he is alert, intelligent, never dull but a bright and amusing companion.

The approved weight given in the standard is five to eleven pounds, the most desirable being six to ten pounds and this gives quite a wide choice of size.

10.3 Griffon Bruxellois (Smooth coated). Bartestree Jasmine (Tazzie).
Photo: John D. Neal.

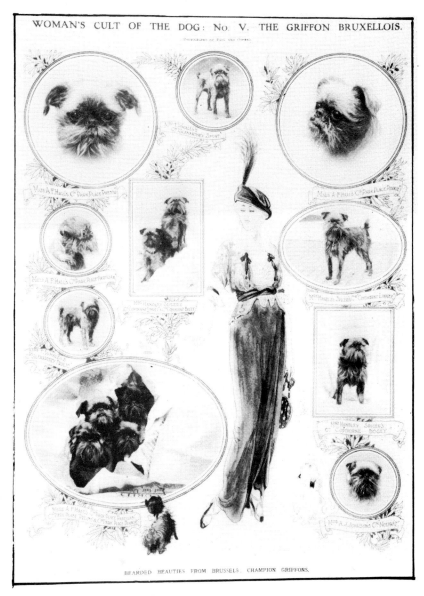

10.4 *Griffon Bruxellois. "Bearded Beauties from Brussels"*
Champion Griffons c. 1913.

10.5 Griffon Bruxellois. A group from Dozmare. Owned by Miss M. Downie.
Photo: Anne Cumbers

Chapter 11

ITALIAN GREYHOUND

One of the early references to the breed, apart from those of centuries ago, came from William Taplin in *The Sportsman's Cabinet* (1804). Although, in common with most other early writers he is not complimentary, his thoughts are of some interest:

"This kind of dog is so little known in England, that it is only necessary for us to offer some observations on its nature in order to prove its existence amidst the group of the canine species which constitute the subject of the present work. In respect to its form, shape, make, and delicate constitution, it may be justly considered truly emblematic of its habitual diffidence and inability. In external appearance the Italian greyhound perfectly resembles the English breed of that description; but from a constitutional want of animation, seems to be entirely destitute of the powers naturally appertaining to that stock. Those who have professedly written upon these subjects, are not known to have introduced anything even plausible or satisfactory upon the origin of this diminutive breed, which seems only calculated to soothe the vanity, and indulge the frivolities of antiquated ladies; some few in this, but more generally in France and Italy, where the breed (as most applicable to the climate) is more universally cultivated. They are so deficient of the spirit sagacity, fortitude, and self-defence of every other sort of the canine race, as not to be able to officiate in the services of domestic alarm or protection; and, in consequence are dedicated only to the comforts of the tea-table, the fire-side carpet, the luxurious indulgencies of the sopha, and the warm lap of the mistress; as a proof of the delicacy of this little

11.1 Italian Greyhound. Ch. Patchwork of Dairylane.
Photo: R. Neal.

11.2 Italian Greyhounds. Ch. Dairylane Premiere Sortie;
Ch. Patchwork of Dairylane; Ch. Dairylane Savoir-Faire.
Photo: R. Neal

animal, it is averred, that if held up by its legs (in the same position as when standing) the texture of the skin is so exceedingly fine, when interveningly opposed to the sun, or a strong light, that the distinct chain of the intestinal canal is truly perceptible to a nice observer."

It is strange that so little early information about its history is given by writers. Many times the breed is mentioned but usually given only a few lines and one is informed that they are dainty, delicate animals of no practical use and require winter clothing; one author tells us they must be wrapped in a rug to venture outside during winter time. William Youatt in 1845 includes the following anecdote:

"It has been said that Frederick the Great of Prussia was very fond of a small Italian greyhound and used to carry it about with him under his cloak. During the seven years' war, he was pursued by a party of Austrian dragoons, and compelled to take shelter, with his favourite, under the dry arch of a bridge. Had the little animal, that was naturally ill-tempered and noisy, once barked, the monarch would have been taken prisoner, and the fate of the compaign and Prussia decided; but it lay perfectly still, and clung close to its master, as if conscious of their mutual danger. When it died it was buried in the gardens of the palace at Berlin, and a suitable inscription placed over its grave."

Youatt thought the breed was deservedly a favourite in the drawing room but inferior in intelligence. Most of the early writers were sporting characters who had little experience of toy dogs although they felt they must be mentioned when writing about dogs, even if it were a difficult task to give more than a brief description. It is refreshing to discover that John Meyrick in *House Dogs and Sporting Dogs* (1861) found the Italian Greyhound worthy of a little more than this which might to some extent redeem its character:

"The little Greyhound is a great favourite from his beauty, grace and liveliness; but he is bred a great deal too slight by the fanciers in this country, to be of use in the field, although I have seen a pure-bred bitch of this kind, imported from Italy by a relative of mine, which would run down rabbits, and was so plucky as to be nearly a match for a Dandie Dinmont Terrier of about her own weight, with which she often had the most sanguinary battles."

J. H. Walsh ("Stonehenge"), though sharing other writers' views upon the delicacy and lack of intelligence of the breed, said that it was one of the most beautifully proportioned animals in creation, being a smooth greyhound in miniature. It has never achieved popularity and as Walsh said, it was not in his time common in this country.

11.3 Italian Greyhound. Ch. Chelanis Finest Kind.
Photo: D. Dalton.

11.4 Italian Greyhound (A Wills' cigarette card).

Despite the lack of numbers, keen fanciers such as Miss H. M. Mackenzie, were able to keep the breed before the public and in 1900 application to the Kennel Club for registration of the Italian Greyhound brought approval and recognition. Herbert Compton, editor of *The Twentieth Century Dog* (1904) gives one of the best accounts of the breed to be found in general dog books and he mentions the part played by Miss Mackenzie, a founder of the first Ladies Kennel Association. The first Secretary of the Italian Greyhound Club was Mrs. B. F. Scarlett who remained in office until 1928 when she was succeeded by Mrs. E. D. Thring, who was also a reputable toy dog judge. These two ladies worked together for many years for the good of the breed. One of the most famous Italian Greyhounds was Ch. *Hero*, bred by Miss Mackenzie and owned by Mrs. Scarlett.

A rather different view of the character of the breed is given by Mrs. Leopold Scarlett in an article contained in Mr. Compton's book and entitled *The Italian Greyhound at Home*:

"Italian Greyhounds are very fond of human society, and as they get on in years prefer it to that of other dogs, particularly young ones, who interfere with their comfort. They are no democrats. My dog, Champion *Hero*, will not look at a servant in a print dress; she goes to the housekeeper's room, and will sit on a silk lap, but she avoids light prints or cottons - they are not "full dress" enough for her! Another dog of this breed which we had was excellent friends with the servants when we were away, but "dropped them" at once on our return.

Then there was *Mab*, who, when I left the house, would not eat except in the dining-room, so the shutters had to be opened for her to have her meal.

The larger specimens course and kill rabbits, and if left to themselves, become arrant poachers. I have known one of ours, of about 10 lbs., run neck and neck with a hare for some distance, being shut off from it by some wire netting. They will hunt a hedgerow in company, like terriers, though they are guided by sight, their hunting scent being defective. At the same time *Hero* always knows when I get a letter from her former mistress, and will pick it out of a packet of twenty others.

Italian Greyhounds require careful treatment and great kindness, especially when puppies, or their nerves may get ruined and their tempers spoiled. They should never be taken up by the scruff of the neck, nor lifted by the forelegs, which is liable to dislocate their shoulder. They require careful handling, and are not in any way suited for children's pets.

11.5 Italian Greyhounds. From an old postcard.

Ch. *Hero* was born in 1896, weighed six and three quarter pounds and was a peach-fawn colour with white chest. Among her many wins was the blue ribbon of the breed, the Marchioness of Waterford's Silver Challenge Cup.

We feel that the rather misleading information on "clothing" needs some clarifying and we cannot do better than to quote Mrs. Annette Oliver, honorary secretary of the Italian Greyhound Club. In her book *Living with Italian Greyhounds* (1983) she states:

"A little coat for the winter time is helpful, but a romp in the garden that time of year does not need such protection. The sensible owner will not force an Italian to venture out for long walks in really cold conditions, or in rain, or strong winds. You only have to feel their warm bodies pressed up against you to appreciate that they lose heat very quickly. It would therefore be foolhardy to expect them to tolerate cold or stormy weather in the same way as a dog with a thicker coat. Perhaps because of their Egyptian origins, the breed are true sun worshippers. During the summer months they will bask in its warmth for hours. In the house, they will follow its progress around your room, perching anywhere to enjoy its rays."

Another requirement peculiar to this toy dog is that, like all types of Greyhound, they have special collars. According to Mrs. Oliver these should be made of soft supple leather to protect the long neck, designed to be wider at the front across the throat. The lead should have a safe clip, never use a slip lead outside the show ring.

The coat is easy to keep in good condition and bathing is only necessary two or three times a year. Hand grooming with a piece of velvet or silk is recommended, stroking from the head towards the tail. Alternatively, Mrs. Shirlee Kalstone, the American grooming expert suggests using a fine quality medium soft bristle brush which will not scratch the dog's skin but will remove the dead hair and dirt. The coat should be soft to the touch, fine and glossy.

There is an enchanting small book about two dogs of this breed called *The Dog in the Tapestry Garden* by Dorothy P. Lathrop published in 1962 by The Macmillan Company, New York. The lonely little Italian Greyhound is joined by a white one with a gold collar which jumped out of a wall tapestry to keep her company. The book is very scarce and quite expensive but well worth buying if a copy can be found.

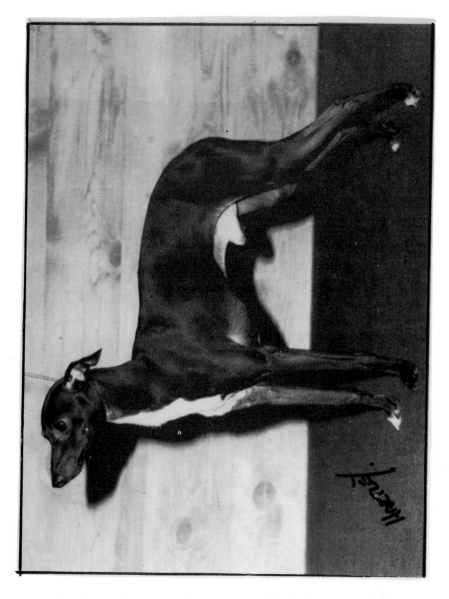

11.6 Italian Greyhound. Ch. Tamoretta Midnite Marauder of Viebrin.
Owned by Mrs. V. Cantrill.
Photo: Hartley

Chapter 12

JAPANESE CHIN

It seems certain that the Japanese Chin originated in China. Dr. Hirth, a well known authority on Chinese and Japanese history has translated the following which is the earliest mention of the Fu-lin dog and dates from the 8th Century:

"During the Nu-to period (618-627 A.D.) The King of Turfan (Turkestan) sent a couple of dogs, male and female, to the Court of China. They were only six inches in height and one foot in length, but highly intelligent."

Lady Samuelson, writing in The Kennel (October 1911), said these were believed to have been the smooth-haired Pekin pugs, and some of them were taken to Japan and there crossed with a native breed which produced the Japanese Chin. She maintained that the name proved the origin, for Shin and Shina are the polite Japanese for Chinese and China.

This lady had been an important breeder of the Chin since about 1890 and related an interesting story. A friend possessed a very valuable and rare book printed in Rome in 1586 from which he translated portions relating to the extensive travels in Europe of four Japanese noblemen. All were aged about eighteen years, and their families had been converted to Christianity some thirty years previously by Father Francis Xavier and the Portugese Jesuits, all of whom were pupils of Loyola.

According to the author of the book, Guido Gaultieri, these young men set out to travel to Europe in 1582, visiting Portugal and Italy. It took them three years, one month and two days, before they reached Lisbon

12.1 Japanese Chin. "Jemima" and "Star."
Photo John Hopwood.

12.2 Japanese Chin. Ch. Momus of Riu Gu.
Photo: Fall.

where they were received with high honours, as they were also at the Court of Spain and finally in Italy. Pope Gregory XIII and the Doge of Venice made them very welcome and innumerable fetes were given in their honour.   `

They were responsible, so it is said, for the introduction of tea into Europe and, more important to our story, for the Japanese Pug.

In the private collection of Prince Borghese at Rome, there was a full-length portrait of Prince Mantio Ito, aged eighteen, nephew of the Daimio of Fiunga, who was the principal envoy of this mission. He was represented in full native dress of richly embroidered silk, with his two swords of ceremony. Great prominence was given in the foreground to his favourite dog, wearing a bejewelled collar. The pet was evidently of Pekingese descent and probably the Japanese Chin of that date descended from those sent from China to Japan in the 7th Century. We understand Prince Mantio Ito gave puppies as presents to the Court of Portugal and the breed is known to have continued to flourish there as late as the time of our Charles I. It is suggested that the spaniels of Charles II were descended from an original pair sent as a royal present to the King of England. This is a particularly significant point as Charles II married Princess Catherine of Braganza (born 1638) a daughter of the King of Portugal.

One of the earliest Japanese shown in England was Mrs. J. Addis's Ch. *Dai Butsu* at Hurlingham in 1894. There is an excellent portrait of her with this dog in C. H. Lane's book *Dog Shows and Doggy People* (1902). Included in the picture is the magnificent silver trophy presented by C. J. Rotherham to the Ladies Kennel Association and named the Rotherham Champion of Champions Cup. Mrs. Addis had seen Japanese Chins in their homeland where they had been bred for centuries and she said "they were kept in cages like rabbits".

Other noted exhibitors in those early days were the Countess of Warwick, Mrs. Loftus Allen of Pekingese fame, Mrs. Hugh Andrews and Mrs. Moss-Cockle. Mrs. McLaren Morrison, who did so much to introduce breeds previously unknown to us into the United Kingdom, also had Japanese. Amongst other large and eminently successful kennels was Mr. Alfred De Rothschild's. His beautiful dogs were housed in The Chalet under the supervision of his kennel keeper, Mrs. Vince. Referring to the dogs in The Chalet, an article in *Our Dogs Supplement* of 4th August, 1904 said:

"Never do these little aristocrats make themselves a nuisance or fret their keeper, and their manners are fit for any lady's boudoir, being most obedient capering full of life and gaiety, in fact life with them is an endless holiday of good times, a picnic of good things, a world of smiles and no frowns."

It was from Mr. Rothschild's kennel that H.M. Queen Alexandra obtained *Punchie*. He and *Billee* were her constant companions and the subject of a miniature painted by Mrs. Gertrude Massey, a well known painter who specialised in children and dogs. Both the Queen and King Edward VII were interested in breeding and exhibiting and kept several breeds in the Royal kennels at Sandringham.

Lady Samuelson was another breeder who visited Japan and imported a number of dogs. Her first was *Nikkho*, a strong and healthy little dog, absolutely self-willed and with a passion for Fox Terriers. Another interesting import was her Ch. *O'Toyo* brought from Nygoya, Japan. Lady Samuelson was visiting Nygoya to see the feudal castle there and knowing there were breeders in the city, took with her a native guide. As a result by the evening the courtyard of her hotel was filled with Japanese men and women bringing their dogs for sale. The outstanding *O'Toyo* came back to the United Kingdom and quickly made his name.

Lady Samuelson commented that in Japan they liked their dogs to have more spaniel shape, longer in body and in outline, whereas in the United Kingdom in 1911 Chins were preferred square and cobby. They are described as very sharp and knowing, very active, bounding about the room like little balls of fluff, graceful and very oriental in appearance, intelligence beaming from their luscious eyes.

Purchasing a Japanese Chin from Japan was not difficult. It was the gruelling sea voyage which was daunting. Many dogs died and others arrived in very poor condition. There was no proper provision for conveying animals and care was minimal.

Although the breed progressed in this country right from the time when an occasional Japanese Chin was smuggled in by sailors, they were very susceptible to disease and distemper wrought havoc in the kennels, many breeders losing their entire kennel more than once. The extreme delicacy of the breed and their complete lack of stamina was a serious problem in those days. This was partly due to poor feeding. The Japanese recommended three small meals a day of cold rice, with a little dried fish sprinkled over, or occasionally a small amount of soup or milk instead of the fish. The dogs were in no condition to fight for their lives against distemper and many succumbed. Breeders were forced to give up the Japanese Chin and turn their attention to the more hardy Pekingese. Eventually some feeding problems were solved, but this took time. As dogs were imported from Japan their new owners were reluctant to

12.3 Japanese Chins from Belgium (a postcard, 1935).

disregard the advice of the Japanese owners who were expected to know what was best for the dogs.

By the early 'twenties the pioneers had been replaced by new breeders including Miss May Tovey of the famous Yevot kennels in Bath; Miss Eileen E. Haig (later Mrs. Craufurd) owner of the winning Rui-Gu kennels where the dogs had complete freedom over a wide area of grassland, Mrs. Stuart Rogers, Miss Jameson and Madame Oosterveen, to name a few.

By this time the problem of delicacy had been largely solved. The author of Les Chiens d'Agrément (1924) Madame Ada Milner of Paris, was devoted to the Japanese and had a large kennel of both Japanese and Pekingese with the prefix of *du Royaume des Fées*. She describes the breed in her book as most attractive and lively, well deserving of all her praise. She says:

"The Japanese are very gay, very lively, and extremely graceful when playing, but with it all they are the quietest toy dog that exists, for they rarely bark; a great advantage in many cases. Some think they are delicate but they are entirely wrong. They are my favourite breed and I have kept them for nearly 24 years and have never found them more delicate than any other breed. I let them have entire liberty running in and out of the garden as they like, in all weathers, even in the snow."

Separate classification was given to the breed by the Kennel Club in 1894 and the breed club was approved on 13th April 1897. Between this time and 1900 at least two attempts were made to divide the dogs by weight over or under seven pounds, but this was not allowed.

According to E. W. Jaquet, then secretary of the Kennel Club who wrote in 1905 *The Kennel Club. A History and Record of its Work*, the Japanese Spaniel Club was amalgamated with the Japanese and Other Asiatic Spaniel Club on 10th October, 1901 under the title of the Japanese and Pekingese Club, but a further application for a division by weight was again not allowed. On 4th March 1902 the Kennel Club directed that the word "spaniel" be deleted from the title of both breeds and in 1904 a separate club for the Pekingese was approved and the Japanese Chin Club was registered.

This is a delightful breed, their long silky coats are not so profuse as to be a problem in grooming, although daily attention is recommended. The desired size is 4 - 7 lbs. They are dainty and graceful and can no longer be considered delicate, they make a very desirable pet.

Chapter 13

KING CHARLES SPANIEL

It is generally believed that the King Charles Spaniel evolved in Europe, possibly in Italy, but the type was fairly common in most continental countries usually under the name of the toy spaniel, by which it is still known in the United States of America.

At the beginning of this century the great authority on these dogs was the Hon. Mrs. Neville Lytton, whose book *Toy Dogs and their Ancestors* was published in 1911. Although the sub-title of this book indicated that it included Pekingese, Japanese and Pomeranians, with brief mention of a few other toy breeds, it was in fact the first book of any note which dealt in detail with the King Charles Spaniel.

It was Mrs. Lytton's opinion that the oldest breed of red and white and possibly also the black and white spaniel originated in China. During the 13th Century the Chinese carried on a brisk trade with Italy. It is likely that these dogs found their way to that country and were crossed with the indigenous dogs, producing the domed heads and pointed noses of the red and white Veronese type, clearly shown in some of the Old Masters. Mrs. Lytton described the red and white spaniel as a pretty Blenheim in general appearance, although later in the book she referred to "the erroneously so-called Blenheim".

The red and white spaniel had existed in Italy two centuries before the birth of the Duke of Marlborough. He was said to have established the Blenheim and it is fairly certain that the spaniels kept by Charles I were

13.1 King Charles Spaniel. Ch. Tudorhurst Royal Revenge.
Photo: Fall.

the larger Cocker and Springer type. Mrs. Lytton quoted *The Shooting Directory* by R. B. Thornhill (1804) in which he stated on page 70:

"Another variety of Cocker, much smaller, is the Marlborough breed, kept by His Grace the Duke of Marlborough; these are red and white, with very round heads, blunt noses, and highly valued by sportsmen.

Our unfortunate monarch, Charles I was much attached to Spaniels, and had always had some of his favourites about him; but these do not appear to have been the small black kind, known by his name, but cockers, as is evident from the pictures of Vandyke, and the print by Sir Robert Strange, after this master, of three of his children, in which they are introduced."

Mrs. Lytton was satisfied that no evidence could be found of the existence of the red and white toy spaniel in England before Henrietta, Duchess of Orleans and sister of Charles II, brought them into this country. When Henrietta died an early death through poisoning, it is probable that Charles II cared for her little dogs and bred them with those she had previously introduced into the English Court which she had visited from France when fifteen years of age.

Therefore there must be some doubt about the views expressed in certain books that red and white toy spaniels were known during, or even before, the reign of Queen Elizabeth I. If this were so it seems likely that these were the same type as those kept by Charles I, which were mentioned in the *Shooting Directory*. They preceded the toy spaniels brought into the country by Henrietta, Duchess of Orleans.

It is clear that Charles I, Charles II and his brother James II, shared a great love for these little dogs, known then as King Charles Spaniels, which were popular at the Court. They were mentioned in the diaries of both Samuel Pepys and John Evelyn. The former disapproved strongly of Charles II's obsession with them, whilst the latter, who was evidently a dog lover and obviously understood their attraction, spoke in the last pages of his diary of the disadvantages of allowing them freedom of the Court.

It is uncertain whether the black and tan spaniel at the Court which had always been accepted without question as the toy King Charles Spaniel, was in fact the favourite of King Charles I. Mrs. Lytton was of the opinion that King Charles owned black and white and particolour spaniels, but never black and tan.

Writing in *The Kennel* (1911) Miss L. Smythe, who must have known Mrs. Lytton well, says that she sought diligently for evidence either way. No contemporary picture of the King with a black and tan spaniel has ever been found; only one of the King with a small particolour dog. Further proof of the existence of particolour toy spaniels at the Court was given in the following advertisement in the *London Gazette* of October 1667:

"Lost in Dean's Yard, Westminster on 26th October last, a young white spaniel about six months old, with a black head, red eyebrows, and a black spot on his back ... belonging to His Highness Prince Rupert. If anyone can bring him to Prince Rupert's lodging in the Stone Galleries at Whitehall, he shall be well rewarded for his pains."

There is reasonable proof of the existence of black toy spaniels at the Court. The first black spaniel on record is in a Mignard picture of Louis of France, later Louis XV. However, it is said that in 1646 William Dobson painted a picture of Sir Charles and Lady Lucas with a black spaniel, but it has not been traced.

According to Miss Smythe, the black and tan spaniels were the favourites of King James II and she quoted Southey as saying:

"King James spaniels are unrivalled in beauty ... black and tan with hair almost approaching silk in fineness; this variety was solely in the possession of the Duke of Norfolk."

The early toy spaniels resembled the Cavalier King Charles Spaniels of today in their length of head. Those of the 19th Century were described as square jawed, heavy and "noseless" in type and were introduced comparatively recently.

The first mention of the abnormally short faces was made by Thomas Pearce ("Idstone") in *The Dog* (1845). There is an overwhelming mass of evidence to prove that pointed noses were the original type of the black and tan and tricolour, although the red and white spaniel had a fairly short face and high skull at all stages. These were similar to the Veronese spaniels, whose description includes: a high domed skull, short pointed nose, a compact and square shape, not too low but not leggy, and tail carried high over the back.

The Toy Spaniel was the only breed with four varieties recorded at the Kennel Club and classified by colour. In 1902 Miss Smythe sought clarification regarding the four colours and asked the Kennel Club whether this was one breed or four - Blenheim, King Charles, Ruby and Prince Charles Spaniels. The Kennel Club regarded them as four varieties of the King Charles Spaniel.

Mrs. L. E. Jenkins, one of the leading breeders at that time, applied a year later for re-classification into five separate colours - Black and Tan, Red or Ruby, Tricolour, Red and White and Marlborough Blenheim. This was not granted, but obviously the colour question continued to be a problem. Finally, late in 1903, a new classification allowed the collective name of the King Charles Spaniel with the following colour divisions: King Charles or Black and Tan; Blenheim, Ruby (or red) and Tricolour.

The Ruby was the last of the four colours and cannot be traced prior to the 19th Century. The first picture of a Ruby is said to be by Landseer and the first written reference to the colour was of a dog called *Dandy* who belonged to Mr. Garwood. It is true that 200 years before Van Dyck painted a picture of Philippe Le Roy with a red spaniel, but this had white on the head and feet, so could hardly be called a whole coloured dog. Mrs. Lytton said that she had traced a whole coloured Ruby spaniel in 1828 which belonged to Mrs. Todd of Newcastle but she had no further details.

It is interesting to find in the *Pall Mall Gazette* of 5th May 1886 a double column devoted to the breed. It was headed "Pets of the Boudoir", and showed pictures of four King Charles spaniels, one of which appeared to be black and all with very domed heads. There was also a basket of three puppies. It gave a very full report of a show at the Royal Aquarium at Westminster which was frequently used for dog shows, eight being held there under Kennel Club regulations during 1886. The whole article, which was unsigned, was about the King Charles Spaniels and a part of it read as follows:

"Just now one of the annexes at the Aquarium is devoted to a collection of these pretty little beasts and here in two long lines of cages may be seen some choice specimens of the breed. Some have brought with them the splendour of the boudoir, and lie nonchalent and impudent on voluptuous couches of yellow and violet, in dainty basinettes worthy of a Royal baby. They gaze longingly through the bars which form their prison, and seem to sigh out - 'from life without freedom, ah' who would not fly?'

Others are couched in less luxury, their silken coats reposing in such humble bedding as hay. Here is a black beauty, a King Charles, with eyes like sloes, the silkiest coat in the world, that might have been spun from gossamer, with a black retreating nose of the correct angle, with trailing ears and sharp mouth. Has he a fault? His coat is too curly. But he is worth a hundred guineas, and is the champion. Sharper and more active is a yellow and white Blenheim, who seems to possess a greater sense of the humorous. And here they sit in the warm spring sun in the best of tempers well disposed and most sociable, proud of chance patronage, welcoming you with a smile and a wag of their bushy tails. Others are shy, and drop their eyes as coyly as a country maiden; others repose at

13.2 *"The Toy Spaniel, 1913."*

full length, with an impudent look in their half-closed eyes, half hidden by their sumptuous draperies - the Nanas of their race. Some yawn, some look bored, others sit on their hind quarters, their tongues lolling out with the heat; one old sage, his snout reclining on a cushion of gold and blue velvet, is a priestly looking dog. Three comic little puppies are playing in a red basket."

King Charles Spaniels are happy, companionable little dogs, enjoy walks and are sporty and playful. In common with most of the toy breeds they thrive better with almost constant human companionship and are very devoted and loyal pets, who love warmth and comfort.

Temperaments differ between the four varieties as their background suggests, but they are usually highly intelligent and can be easily taught and trained as they are anxious to please. They are sometimes rather possessive and fairly quick tempered, conscious of their place in the pecking order with other dogs in the family, and although not fighters are usually determined to keep that order. Like most of the toy breeds they are inclined to be nervous of children and are not really suitable as a child's pet.

The long silky coat requires daily grooming but one is amply rewarded by the elegance and beauty of the dog. As four colours are recognised by the Kennel Club it is not difficult to find one to please, from Black and Tan, Tricolour, Blenheim or Ruby. Weight varies between eight and fourteen pounds.

13.3 King Charles Spaniel. Ch. Corosco Peerless Peter of Oakridges.
Owned by Mrs. Mollie Castle.

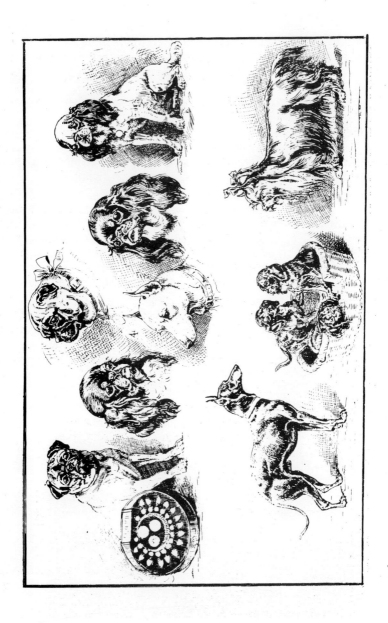

13.4 Toy Dog Show at the Royal Aquarium, London. 1866.

Chapter 14

LOWCHEN (LITTLE LION DOG)

This is one of the least known of our toy dogs, the first importation coming from Germany as recently as 1968. It is a very old breed, originating in the Mediterranean countries and closely linked with the Havanese and Bichon group which also included the Maltese.

It was not unknown in the United Kingdom and Lillian C. Smythe ("Lady Betty") writing in *The Kennel*, June 11th 1911, has this to say:

"I am indebted to Mrs. Kennedy for the inspection of a most delightful old book, Bewick's *History of Quadrupeds*, printed at Newcastle-on-Tyne in 1791: which gives, very pleasantly, and all with the long ss, *(the long shaped ancient form of s.)* much lore on the subject of dogs. Toy Dogs naturally have but little space allotted to them; and it names four only. "The King Charles Dog", which it describes as 'an idle but innocent companion'; and refers to its curled hair and web feet. The Pyrame-dog, black with reddish legs; and the "Shock-dog", a diminutive creature, almost hid in the great quantity of its hair which covers it from head to foot."

But of chief interest is this reference: 'Another variety is the lion- dog, so called from the shaggy hair which covers the head and all the fore-part of the body; whilst the hinder part is quite smooth, saving a tuft of hair at the end of the tail. This species is become extremely rare.' Mrs. Kennedy says: 'Can this be the Pekingese?' And an answer may be found in the accompanying illustration from another old book, of "The Lion Dog".

14.1 Lowchen (Little Lion Dog). Ch. Littlecourt Acajou.
Photo: Diane Pearce.

14.2 Lowchen (Little Lion Dog). Ch. Jingle Joys Black Cinder of Rumawill.
Photo: Fall.

The breed was known by William Youatt in 1845. In *The Dog* he said:

"The Lion Dog is a diminutive likeness of the noble animal whose name it bears. Its head, neck, shoulders, and forelegs down to the very feet, are covered with long, wavy, silky hairs. On the other parts of the dog, it is so short as scarcely to be grasped, except that on the tail there is a small bush of hair. The origin of this breed, is not known; it is, perhaps, an intermediate one between the Maltese and the Turkish dog."

John Meyrick in *House Dogs and Sporting Dogs* (1861) had this to say:

"It is a common pet on the continent, where he is often crossed with the Barbet. He is generally shaved to increase the fancied resemblance to the Lion, which the long wavy hair on his head, back and shoulders gives him. It was probably in ignorance of this custom, that Youatt describes the hair on the rest of his body as being very short; the fact being that the whole body is covered with hair almost equally long with that on the forepart, like the Maltese Terrier, which this little dog much resembles in colour, shape and size."

Meyrick adds an interesting footnote. In the past the services of the taxidermist were in demand, which was probably fortunate as in certain museums one can see an actual well known dog, an ancestor of our dogs of today. Meyrick says:

"A beautiful stuffed specimen may be seen, by those curious in the points of this breed, in the window of Mr. Buffon's shop in the Strand. As in most stuffed dogs, however, the face is a good deal distorted. I may observe that this will invariably take place in stuffed specimens from the shrinking of the nose in the act of drying, unless that part is cut off and replaced by a nose modelled after the original in properly coloured wax."

H. D. Richardson in *Dogs, their Origins and Varieties* (1851) thinks that the breed may have resulted from a cross between the small Barbet and the naked Turk. He adds that it is "A very rare variety and useless". Charles Hamilton-Smith in *The Naturalists Library* (1840) also found it "extremely rare".

Russia has been suggested as the original home of the Lowchen but no evidence of this has been found and Robert Leighton's assertion that it was more likely to be found in Germany and Holland seems feasible.

Neither is there any evidence that it had anything to do with the Pekingese often referred to as the Lion Dog of China, which of course prompted Mrs. Kennedy to wonder if Bewick's Lion Dog could have been a Pekingese. The Hon. Mrs. Neville Lytton mentions this similarity in name in *Toy Dogs and their Ancestors (1911)* but states that she failed to find any connection at all between the breeds.

Dr. Walther, said to have been one of the most conscientious fanciers in about 1817, preferred to call the Lion Dog by its Latin name of Leoninus. He said the name was natural as it was due simply to the method of clipping the hair to make this little dog look "lion-like".

The name of the dog is not now in question, as it is officially recognised by the Kennel Club as the Lowchen (Little Lion Dog).

One of the few breeders in France who met with success was Madame Max conninck. We believe that she also bred the Havanese one of which, *Polka de Dieghem*, later the property of Madame Malenfew, was awarded a first prize under a judge from the United Kingdom, Frederick Gresham. So it is reasonable to assume that he also was familiar with the Lowchen, although he does not mention the breed in the small book which he wrote at the end of the last century. However, when writing about the Maltese he says that in some parts of the world it is known as the Lion Dog of Malta.

The Lowchen was sometimes shown before the first World War, but it was contended that they were simply bad coloured Maltese with a wavy, instead of a straight coat and with lemon markings. Some owners had resorted to clipping the coats to enable them to exhibit the dogs as Lion Dogs. The size was similar to the Maltese, although many were heavier.

According to Freda McGregor writing in *Our Dogs* in 1984, it was thanks to Madame Bennert of Brussels that this rare breed was kept alive during the Second World War. Madame Bennert's interest in the toy breeds was widespread and in *The Papillon 'Butterfly' Dog* (1985) we note that she was a Belgian delegate to the Congress held at Lille in 1934, organised by the International Union of Papillon Clubs (UNICLEPPA).

The first imported Lowchens to reach this country from Germany in 1968 were from Dr. Hans Rickert to Mrs. E. M. Stenning, followed by two from the same kennel to Mrs. Elisha Banks who bred the first champion inethe breed, Ch. *Cluneen Adam Adamant*. The first bitch champion was Int. Ch. *Littlecourt Emma*, bred by Mrs. McGregor from Mrs. Banks's dogs.

In its natural state the Lowchen has a long, soft wavy coat, fine and silky. To retain the lion-like outline this has to be kept clipped. It has been suggested that some pet owners may prefer to keep the long coat, thus making the dog look like a miniature version of the Bearded Collie. We feel that it would be a pity to alter this unique little dog, but it would be a matter for each individual owner to decide whether the time spent on additional grooming to save clipping, was worthwhile.

It is a hardy little dog, sturdily built, 10 to 13 inches at the withers, with gaily carried tail and a sweet expression. Any colour is acceptable. In temperament the breed is naturally affectionate and good tempered, showing no signs of aggression. They make lively and intelligent pets.

We have been unable to trace any monographs on this breed, but they are briefly mentioned in many of the more recently published general dog books.

14.3 Lowchen (Little Lion Dog). Eng. & Sw. Ch. Jinglejoys Bright Baron of Littlecourt. Owned by Mrs. F. McGregor.
Photo: Dalton

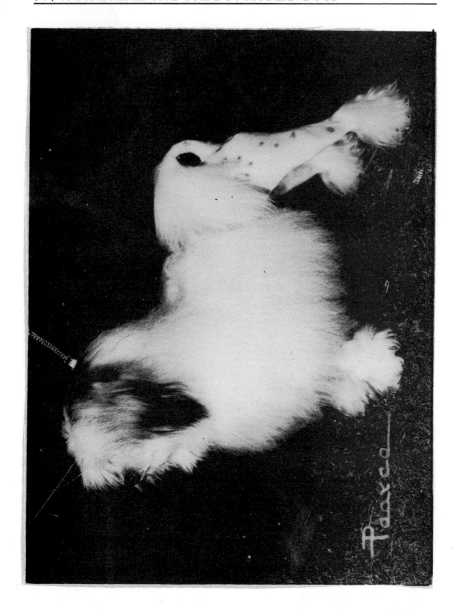

14.4 Lowchen (Little Lion Dog). Ch. Cleeview Gunther of Littlecourt. Owned by Mrs. F. McGregor.
Photo: Pearce.

Chapter 15

MALTESE

This little Bichon-type dog, formerly erroneously called the Maltese Terrier, is certainly one of the oldest toy breeds.

Captain Thomas Brown in *Biographical Sketches and Authentic Anecdotes of Dogs* (1829) refers to Strabo (circa A.D.25):

"Strabo informs us that 'there is a town in Pachynus, a promontory of Sicily (called Meleta) from whence are transported many fine little dogs, called Melitae Canes. They were accounted the jewels of women: but now the said town is possessed by fishermen, and there is no such reckoning made of those tender little dogs, which are not bigger than common ferrets or weasels; yet are they not small in understanding, nor unstable in their love to men, for which cause they are also nourished tenderly for pleasure."

Captain Brown continues:

"He is a beautiful little animal, and is much esteemed by the fair sex in Malta and other islands of the Mediterranean. He is extremely affectionate to his owner, but generally peevish and ill-tempered to strangers."

Edward C. Ash in *Dogs, their History and Development* (1927), whilst agreeing that the breed goes back into antiquity states:

"It is curious that early works dealing with Malta give no mention of the far-famed Maltese dog, and it may be that it was considered by these travellers of little importance, or else was not at that time kept on the island.

15.1 Maltese. Ch. Ellwin Sweet Charity.
Photo: Dave Freeman.

The latter is more probable, for in 1804 Louis de Boisgelin, Knight of Malta, writes:

"There was formerly a breed of dogs in Malta with long silky hair which were in great demand in the time of the Romans; but have for some years past greatly dwindled and indeed are become almost extinct. "

The type was mentioned by Dr. Johannes Caius in a treatise written for his friend, Conrad Gesner, to include in his work on natural history. Caius, physician-in-chief to Queen Elizabeth I was a noted scholar and founder of the Gonville and Caius College, Cambridge. He published the treatise in 1570 under the title of *De Canibus Britannicis*, which was the second dog book recorded, the first being the famous *Boke of St. Albans*. Caius listed recognised breeds of that time under some curious names, most of which are decipherable; he went into some detail classifying the dog in sections according to their employment as shepherd's dogs, hunting dogs and so on, his third group being the "Spaniel gentle" or "Comforter".

Shortly after publication a scholar by the name of Abraham Fleming interpreted and translated this Latin treatise into English. Of the third group which was: "Of the delicate, neate, and pretty kind of dogges called the Spaniel gentle, or the comforter, in Latine Melitaeous or Fotor" he commented as follows:

"There is, besides those which we haue already delivered, another sort of gentle dogges in this our English soyle but exempted from the order of the residue, the Dogges of this kinds doth Callimachus call Melitaeos, of the Iseland Melita, in the sea of Sicily (what at this day is named Malta), an Iseland indeede famous and renoumed, with courageous and puisaunt souldiours valliauntly fighting under one banner of Christ their vnconquerable captaine) where this kind of dogges had their principal beginning."

Clearly the Bichon type of dog was known in England in the 16th Century.

The origins and history of the Maltese have been dealt with in some depth, notably by Virginia T. Leitch of the Jon Vir kennels in the United States of America in her book *The Maltese Dog* published in 1953 and revised by Dennis Carno. Mrs. Leitch traces the breed back for centuries and it is undoubtedly one of the oldest, if not the oldest dog known to have existed as a distinct breed. In this country Miki Iveria writing in *Maltese Dogs the Jewels of Women* (1979) shows illustrations of Bichon-type dogs of the 15th Century. In consequence we leave details

15.2 Maltese. Ch. Ellwin Touch of Magic.

of early origins to those authorities and proceed to the dogs of the 19th Century.

The Maltese is one of the few toy dogs mentioned in 19th Century books, not as a rarity but as one of the breeds to be encountered in this country. Princess Victoria owned one called *Fluffy* and at the same time owned a pet dove. Mrs. Gertrude Massey, the miniaturist who specialised in animals and was a great favourite at the Court, painted these two, *Fluffy* and *Dovey*, in a "unique miniature". The writer of *Dogs in Miniature* described *Fluffy* as a ball of soft hair white as snow, and *Dovey* as pure white and very wise-looking, befitting his age for he had been the Princess's companion for twenty three years and followed her about just like a dog. There was no rivalry between the two, the dove perching on the head of the Maltese or between his paws.

One of the most enthusiastic early fanciers was Mr. R. Mandeville of Southwark whom Robert Leighton called the founder of the Maltese. Two of his dogs called *Fido* and *Lily* were said to have been the most perfect representatives of the breed during the decade between 1860 and 1870 and were shown at Birmingham, Islington, the Crystal Palace and Cremorne Gardens, all being important shows. Lady Gifford was the owner of *Hugh*, a particularly lovely white dog with a "coat like floss silk, white as the driven snow" and dark pigmentation. He weighed between four and five pounds. His picture appeared in colour with a large Pomeranian dog in Vero Shaw's *The Illustrated book of the Dog* (1879/81).

Mrs. McLaren Morrison, whose name was familiar to all toy breed fanciers was also interested in the Maltese. In those days the breed remained in a few hands. Strangely several times mention has been made of the "snappishness" of the Maltese, but Robert Leighton believed this was not an innate characteristic and could easily be controlled by early training. He deplored the custom of keeping the Maltese "enclosed in tin canisters" so that they might remain diminutive; he stated that even in the early 20th Century some were kept tied up in bags so that their feet "may not have room to scratch and their coats may not be soiled". He felt that the beauty of a silky white coat should not be kept at the sacrifice of its owner's physical comfort and freedom.

These dogs, which should not exceed ten inches at the withers, need care in grooming. A pin or natural bristle brush is recommended and a half-fine, half-medium style comb. It is essential to groom daily and to take particular care to keep the beard hair clean, not allowing it to become discoloured after feeding. Keeping this small dog in condition, grooming, and preparing for show, needs time and care. The pet owner is advised to discuss care and management with the breeder before buying a dog. Those who have the time and enjoy the pleasure of owning one of these beautiful dogs will feel amply rewarded for the work entailed in keeping it in a state of perfection.

The Maltese Club was approved for registration by the Kennel Club on 2nd July, 1903 and in 1987 is still the only club in the United Kingdom which caters for this breed.

15.3 Maltese. Ch. Ellwin Petite Chanteus.
Photo: Diane Pearce.

Chapter 16

MINIATURE PINSCHER

This smart little dog is of German descent, a member of the dwarf Pinscher/Schnauzer family and was sometimes known as the Zwerg Reh Pinscher as he was said to resemble the small red deer which used to frequent the forests in Germany. Tracing the evolution of the breed is difficult, but it was first officially mentioned by name by Dr. H. G. Reinchenbach in 1836 who stated that the dogs were most often black or red. He suggests they might have been bred from a cross between the Pug and the Dachshund, or maybe the Italian Greyhound and the Dachshund, all three of which are old breeds.

Viva Leone Ricketts in her book *The Complete Miniature Pinscher* (1972) says she is inclined to agree with this supposition and considers the Italian Greyhound cross with a Dachshund the more likely. Her opinion is that the Pinscher is a very old breed, although documentation dates only from the early 19th Century. This point of view was shared by Margaret R. Bagshaw in *Pet Miniature Pinscher* (1958) who considers that the breed could have been known for centuries in the Scandinavian countries, Europe and Asia. She says that skeletons unearthed near lake dwellings in Switzerland support her theory. Both are certain that this toy pinscher pre-dates the Doberman Pinscher and with this we also agree. There is a certainty about the origin of the Doberman in some quarters which is not encountered in other breeds.

This dog was produced by Louis Dobermann of Apolda in Thueringia, Germany, about 1890 and we understand from Henry P. Davis, editor of

16.1 Miniature Pinscher. Ch. Lionlike Red Fire Fox.
Photo: Diane Pearce.

16.2 Miniature Pinscher. Ch. Lionlike Black Reno.

The Modern Dog Encyclopaedia (1949) that it was Dobermann's ambition to breed a large dog. Henry Davis says:

"That is, a dog built upon Terrier lines and owning a Terrier's grace and agility, but one with the strength of a typical German working shepherd, or draft dog. The dog he visioned would look much like a five pound Miniature Pinscher but would be some 15 times heavier."

It is believed by Viva Leone Ricketts that the larger type of German Shepherd and the Rottweiler were used to produce the Doberman Pinscher, and later perhaps the Manchester Terrier was certainly used by breeders. It is established that the first typical Doberman was produced and registered in the German stud book in 1890, long after the Miniature Pinscher was generally accepted.

There is no evidence that the Miniature Pinscher was "bred down" from the Doberman, in fact this popular belief is shown by the facts to be a misconception.

Apart from those dogs exported to the United States of America in the early 1930's, the breed was little known outside Europe until 1950.

In the United Kingdom the breed club was founded and recognised by the Kennel Club in 1955. One of the first kennels in this country was the *Hayclose* owned by John and Peggy Stott, whose foundation bitch, *Davina of Tavey*, was bred in the United Kingdom. A very successful kennel belonged to Mr. Lionel Hamilton-Renwick and many champions held his *Birling* prefix. Among the great Miniature Pinschers from this kennel was Ch. *Birling Painted Lady*, Ch. *Birling Wawocan Constellation*, her sire, and Ch. *Birling High Jinks*.

The Miniature Pinscher has an outstanding personality commented upon by a number of writers. Viva Leone Ricketts says of him:

"His eagerness to please his owner makes him easy to train, and he rates highly in obedience training and competition. His intelligence is high, and he quickly figures out the odds against him and acts accordingly... He is an ideal house dog and companion, sturdy enough even when quite young to be a companion and playmate for young children."

Dr. William A. Bruette and Kerry V. Donnelly in *The Original Complete Dog Book* (1979) agree:

"An alert, intelligent breed with confidence enough to approach dogs many times their size without any hint of fear or submissiveness. If needed will protect their home ... He has strong jaws and powerful teeth ... is more feared by a prowler than a burglar alarm."

His smooth, glossy coat is easily kept in order and is usually a solid red or black with sharply defined tan markings, solid brown, or chocolate with rust or yellow markings. His tail is docked.

For those changing from a larger breed who may find the toy spaniel type too quiet and docile, this game little dog might appeal as an excellent companion and house dog. It should be remembered, however, that he is very lively and active with all the instincts of a sportsman's dog despite his small size.

Chapter 17

PAPILLON (BUTTERFLY DOG)

The Papillon has a continental background but is probably of Far Eastern origin, and it has changed very little over the years. It is a charming little dog which has recently become one of the leading toy breeds in this country.

There are two varieties. Those with the erect ears are called Papillons and the variety with dropped ears is called the Phalène". The two words are French, the former meaning "butterfly" and the latter "moth".

This was a little known breed in the United Kingdom until the early 1920's, although it had gained popularity at the Courts on the continent. France particularly was one of the European countries which had a wide variety of dogs for the chase. Many of these breeds have died out, but nevertheless the desire for dainty little pet dogs seems to have been much more prevalent there than in this country. We read of the passion of Henri III of France for these little dogs from Lyons and the elaborate arrangements he made for their care and management.

Little is known about the pet dogs at Court between 1589 and Louis XV's reign, but we do know that his Royal favourite, Madame de Pompadour, had a pet Papillon called *Inez* and many other figures in Europe and Scandinavia favoured these dogs. There is an interesting picture in the Louvre, Paris, of Henriette-Anne Stuart, Duchess of Orleans and sister-in-law to Louis XVI, holding a perfect tiny Phalène.

These small continental spaniels were also known in Prussia, certain parts of Russia and in the Scandinavian countries where the breed is firmly established today.

In view of its popularity abroad it seems puzzling that this type of toy spaniel hardly appeared in the United Kingdom before the 20th Century although it was a familiar sight in Old Masters for several hundred years. However, in the 1920's a stalwart but small band of enthusiasts introduced the Papillon into this country and it was largely due to the courage of Mrs. M. B. Cooper, Mrs. Gordon Gratrix, Mrs. C. M. Hunter, Mrs. I. Ashcroft and others that support was found and a breed club with Mrs. Hunter as chairman, was formed in 1923. When the club celebrated its Diamond Jubilee in April 1983 with a show and dinner, she was the only one of the pioneers left. Sadly she died a few months later.

In pre-war days there were a number of exports from this country, many of which went to the United States of America. Although the American Kennel Club did not officially recognise a breed club for the Papillon until 1935, the Papillon Club of America, founded in 1930 flourished, but the breed was spread somewhat thinly across the continent. This popularity has been maintained and further extended into Canada. Unfortunately in most countries the attractive drop-eared variety, the Phalène, has been superseded by the more dominant erect eared dogs, although it has never completely died out. Only in Sweden has the variety made any real progress. In that country, in accordance with the regulations of the Fédération Cynologique Internationale which drew up the *standard* of points used in many countries, the Phalène is separately registered with the Swedish Kennel Club.

As a pet the breed has many qualifications, not least its beauty. A well cared for Papillon is a joy to own. The long, silky coat is easy to look after, markings and colouring are attractive; it has longer legs than many toy dogs and its delicate hare feet do not bring much mud or dampness into the house. It is inexpensive and easy to feed, usually obedient and sweet tempered unless teased. In fact an ideal pet, although the fine bone and small stature do not make the smaller Papillon suitable for households with young children unless there is sensible supervision of the children and the dog.

As a breed they are alert, quick and impulsive and for this reason one has to be prepared to watch over them more carefully than might be necessary for the more placid type of dog. They are adaptable and will accept most conditions. They enjoy a walk on the lead, but are perfectly happy in the garden. Although as adults they are good walkers this is not a necessity if the garden is safely fenced for them to have their freedom there. Although a great deal of patience and time is necessary to train them in competitive obedience work they seem to enjoy it and work well. Their size can be a slight handicap but even so a number of Papillons in this country have been trained to a high grade.

If given the extra care common to all long coated small breeds it is reasonably hardy. The average life span usually exceeds twelve years and will probably reach fourteen or fifteen years. A brief daily grooming, with special care to ensure that there is no matting of the hair on the ears, legs and tail, will keep the dog looking at its best. A coat regularly brushed will keep in clean condition without constantly bathing the dog.

For anyone looking for an easily managed and intelligent companion this is an ideal breed.

17.1 Papillon. Ch. Fircrest Filemon.
Photo: Fall.

17.2 Papillons. A Group of Papillons. L. to R. Ch. Fircrest Filemon,
Ch. Fircrest Fantutti, Ch. Gerlil Rhett Butler and Ch. Miss Anne of
Daffodilwoods.
Photo: Fall

Chapter 18

PEKINGESE

The story of this breed, its Imperial background in the Summer Palace in Peking and the mixture of fact and legend must have made some contribution to the fascination of this little dog which immediately attracted the attention of all toy dog enthusiasts. In her book *Pekingese Guide* (1969) Frances Sefton repeats the charming legend of the origins of the Pekingese:

"Once upon a time in the land of Korea there lived a lion. But he was a happy lion. He had fallen deeply in love with a tiny monkey. The monkey, sensible as are all of the feminine sex, pointed out to the lion how ridiculous was the idea of marriage, because they were so different in size.

The lion was inconsolable. He pleaded with the Lord Buddha to help him. Could not the Lord Buddha make him small like the pretty monkey, so that she might accept his favours? The Lord Buddha was impressed by the great love the lion had for the monkey - so great that for her he was willing to sacrifice his strength and power. And so he granted the lion's prayer but let him keep his great courage, his big heart, and his majesty.

The lion and the monkey were married and from this union came the Pekingese - with the form, the heart, the courage and the dignity of the lion and the impudent face, the intelligence and sense of the monkey."

In our opinion the origin of the breed probably has some link with the spaniels of Tibet but is buried in time and difficult to prove. It was said

18.1 Pekingese. Ch. Micklee Roc's Ru Ago.
Photo: Keith Lloyd.

18.2 Pekingese. Pekehuis Joybell.
Photo: Fall.

in China that a royal breed of dog from Manchuria had existed from time immemorial in the Imperial Palace in Peking.

Proof is forthcoming in the 19th Century and the history books describe the sacking of the Summer Palace in Peking which took place in 1860.

It is known that Lord John Hay, at that time Captain of H.M.S. Odin and later an Admiral of the Fleet, brought the first two Pekingese into England. The dark red dog with a black muzzle was called *Schlorff* who lived to be eighteen years old and died in his possession. There was also a black and white bitch, *Hytien*, whom he gave to his sister the Duchess of Wellington and she was the forerunner of the Pekingese dogs at Strathfieldsaye.

With Lord John Hay was another naval officer, Sir George Fitzroy, a relative of the Duchess of Richmond, who took two of the dogs and gave them to her. These two were small, five to six pounds in weight.

Mr. T. Douglas Murray in *The Pekingese* said that this classes them among the "sleeve dogs", of which the Dowager Empress possessed two, and these tiny dogs were highly prized in the Imperial Palace.

The term "sleeve dog" had become customary in the western world to describe any small Pekingese. The interpretation given by His Excellency the Chinese Minister in London, Lord Li Ching-fong, at the beginning of this century was different. His Excellency, writing in *The Pekingese* (1912) said:

"When I was in Pekin, I discovered that ladies were very fond of keeping tiny dogs, and the smaller these are the higher is their value. Some of them are not more than six inches in length, and can be carried about in the bosum. This breed is called "Habba", known in this country as the "sleeve dog". Not only are they very rare, but, also, naturally very expensive. On my arrival in this country, I was agreeably surprised to find that such dogs were very popular, especially with ladies. Not only are they highly prized here, but I soon learned that societies are in existence having their object the improvement of the breed."

In his book *The Pekingese* (1936) Mr. Edward C. Ash suggests that the name originated through the Chinese habit of carrying these small specimens in their sleeves.

The fifth of those taken from the apartment of the Emperor's aunt, who it was said, committed suicide on the approach of the troops, was a tiny fawn and white bitch which was presented to H.M. Queen Victoria by General J. Hart Dunne. Although it has always been assumed that *Looty* lived at Windsor, the Queen appears to have had little knowledge

18.3 Pekingese. Ch. Ebernoe After Thought.
Photo: Marc Henrie, ASC.

of her. In 1935 when preparing his book Edward C. Ash endeavoured to substantiate the presumption. He says:

"We also know that Her Majesty Queen Victoria graciously accepted the fawn and white one. Mr. T. Douglas Murray tells us that it was so small that General Dunne had informed him that it would sleep curled up in his forage cap."

However, Mr. Ash was unable to find a letter from General Dunne to Her Majesty or any mention of *Looty* in Queen Victoria's published letters. He wrote to the Librarian at Windsor Castle, hoping to find some note made by the Queen or a letter or description of the dog, but no information came to light.

Thirty-two years later when Rumer Godden was researching for her book she was more fortunate. She published in *The Butterfly Lions* (1977) a facsimile letter signed by General Dunne, then Captain of the 99th Regiment. This was undated but it is assumed it was sent in 1861. It describes the "little creature" as most affectionate and intelligent. It adds the dog was used to being treated as a pet and it was with this hope that he had brought it from China to present to Her Majesty and the Royal family. Miss Godden says in Source Notes that this information was obtained from the unpublished correspondence in the Royal Archives at Windsor. *Looty's* life-sized portrait was painted by a pupil of Landseer, Friedrich William Keyl in 1861 and clearly reproduced in Lillian C. Smythe's *The Pekingese*.

The portrait was hung in the Royal Academy in 1862.

Although Queen Victoria left no notes on this dog, *Looty's* death at Windsor in 1872 when in the care of Mrs. Cowley was recorded.

In 1893 Captain Loftus Allen brought the grey brindle, *Pekin Peter* to England. It seems likely that Mrs. Loftus Allen, a sister- in-law of the Duchess of Richmond, was the first exhibitor of a Pekingese when she showed him at Chester the following year.

Two years later Captain Loftus Allen brought two black Pekingese from China, the first of this colour in the country. The bitch, *Pekin Princess*, was a clear black. In *The Perfect Pekingese* (1912) Mrs. Loftus Allen said these dogs came from the Palace itself and were obtained from an employee of the Imperial Household by Mr. Frank Maillard who, in turn, procured them from a brother of his native "boy".

Mr. T. Douglas Murray related in an article entitled "The Ancient Palace Dogs of China" published in *The Pekingese* (1909) that Sir Chaloner Alabaster the British Consul-General in Canton, presented him with a Pekingese puppy and told him it was a great rarity. During his thirty years residence in China he had never before seen one in Canton, or indeed outside Peking.

Mr. Murray said that after a further five years of endeavour he succeeded in obtaining a pair of Pekingese from the Palace in 1896. These were named *Ah Cum* (who lived until 1905) and a bitch, *Mimosa* who survived him by four years. *Ah Cum* can be seen at the British Museum at Tring, an example of the skill of the taxidermists of that era. These, together with Mrs. Loftus Allen's small kennel of Pekingese, some of which were being exhibited, were the foundation stock of the breed in this country.

The year 1896, was the turning point in favour of the breed. Mrs. Loftus Allen showed *Prince* and *Princess* as "foreign spaniels" at the Pet Dog Show at the Royal Aquarium, Westminster and the Ladies Kennel Association Show in Holland Park, London. A year later Lady Algernon Gordon Lennox showed a Goodwood dog, *Joss*, in the foreign dog class as a Pekingese Pug or Spaniel. Crufts Dog Show did not provide a class for the breed until 1900. The first Pekingese to attain full championship was Mrs. Loftus Allen's *Goodwood Lo*, followed by *Goodwood Chun*.

The Japanese Spaniel Club registered with the Kennel Club on 13th April 1897 drew up the first Pekingese *standard* in 1896. In 1901 this club amalgamated with the Japanese and Other Asiatic Spaniel Club under the title of the Japanese and Pekingese Club. By 1904 the popularity of the Pekingese had risen by leaps and bounds. Their owners, who were also members of the Japanese and Pekingese Club, felt that a suitable time had arrived to separate from the club and to form themselves into an independent body. The Pekingese Club was founded by Mr. George Brown, a member of the consular service in China, Mrs. Loftus Allen, Mrs. Ashton Cross who, with her three daughters established a magnificent kennel of the Alderbourne Pekingese and several other interested fanciers.

The breed *standard* was based on the points laid down by the original importers, aided by Sir Chihchen Lufengluh, Sir Halliday Macartney, also a member of the Chinese Government Service, Baron Speck von Stermberg and the German Minister in Peking. The maximum weight was given as ten pounds.

At this time owing to their increasing popularity some anxiety was felt about type. Lady Algernon Gordon Lennox said that scores of Pekingese in the show ring had lost all resemblance to the Palace type for which the maximum weight had been fixed at ten pounds. This maximum had more recently been raised to eighteen pounds, followed by the lifting of any restriction on weight, which Lady Algernon thought had led to

"LION DOGS, SUN DOGS, AND SLEEVE DOGS": THE PERFECT PEKINGESE.

18.4 Pekingese. "The Perfect Pekingese. 1913."

confusion about the true type. She felt that the Palace dog and the larger dog known as the Pekin Spaniel should be kept distinct. She quoted a letter from Lord John Hay, written several years before:

"Now there is another breed which is confounded with the Palace dog; they present the same characteristics; appearance very similar, and disposition equally charming, but they are *much larger*; they are also called Peking Spaniels; but they are as different breeds originally, I feel sure, as a Pegu pony is from an English hunter; they are seldom so well provided with hair on the feet, and the trousers do not go down far enough; also the hair on the stomach and sides does not grow long enough."

Mrs. Ashton Cross resigned from the committee of the Pekingese Club and with Lady Algernon Gordon Lennox founded the Pekin Palace Dog Association in 1908, whose breed *standard* varied slightly from that of the Pekingese Club in an effort to preserve the true type.

From this stage the breed quickly gained in strength and became the most popular toydog for many decades, before giving way recently to the Yorkshire Terrier and the Cavalier King Charles Spaniel.

This popularity spread slowly to the United States of America. The American artist, Miss Katherine A. Carl travelled to Peking in 1904 to paint a portrait of the Empress Dowager and from her book *With the Dowager Empress of China* we have learnt a great deal abut the Pekingese which would have otherwise been lost.

In later years breeders of most long coated dogs have concerned themselves with the quality and length of coat, none more so than the Pekingese breeders. There is no denying that the coats are magnificent. However it is a pity that the distinctive lion shaped body, of major importance to the breed, is now completely covered in a massive flowing coat nearly reaching the ground. This tends to make the dog look a little dull and quiescent. It also raises doubts in the minds of those looking for a reasonably easy to manage pet when they realise the work entailed to produce such an immaculately groomed aristocrat who looks as if he has never left the imagined silken cushions.

Before purchasing a Pekingese enquiries should be made about the proper grooming procedure. This way it is possible to decide whether time allows the dog to be kept in proper condition which is equally important for show or as a pet. A neglected and matted coat is uncomfortable for the dog and embarrassing for the owner.

The Pekingese is far from being a lap dog as popularly supposed. Given the opportunity he is one of the most sporting toydogs and likes nothing better than country walks, although he can be adaptable and willing to curb his desires if necessary to live more sedately in the town.

He has the true Asian outlook. In character he is calm and dignified, not noisy; perhaps too self-reliant to respond quickly to orders. This trait is common also in most Tibetan breeds and sometimes noticed in the Japanese Chin. If called away from some particularly interesting occupation he will often look up, wag his tail to show he has heard and decide whether or not immediate response is necessary. He is loyal and affectionate and courageous by nature. Although not foolishly impulsive he is adventurous and will often take advantage. He will walk briskly with purpose and confidence and have a look around. He is full of self-importance, highly intelligent and a delightful and amusing companion, but if the "clinging" type of pet is preferred he will probably be too independent.

Those who scorn the breed before acquiring some knowledge of it will find the Pekingese does not demand luxury and is not forever "snorting" which are two of the usual misconceptions about this sporting, hardy little dog who makes such an ideal pet.

18.5 A Pekingese and her puppies.

18.6 Sleeve Pekingese. Old Pekin Sarah Jane. Owned by Mrs. K. Pemberton.
Photo: Hartley.

14.7 Pekingese. Ch. Bimbo of Fewling. Owned by Mrs. F. Elkan.
Photo: Fall

Chapter 19

POMERANIAN

Most monologues on the Pomeranian give little space to early history and begin with the 20th Century. We appreciate that unconfirmed statements about the earlier days do not contribute greatly to knowledge but they are sometimes of interest, so we have delved a little further back to the early part of the 19th Century.

We looked at some of the research done by Mr. G. M. Hicks, M.A. for *The Pomeranian* (1906) in which he gave his valid reasons for stating that the origins of the Pomeranian lie in eastern Europe. Before doing so we will examine the reason for our own conviction that the Pomeranian was known in this country long before 1800.

In 1803/4 the third book dealing entirely with the dog was published in London. This was: *The Sportsman's Cabinet, or a Correct Delineation of the various dogs used in the Sports of the Field*. It was written by "A Veteran Sportsman" who was in fact William Taplin. Although we may find his summing up of the character of the Pomeranian a little harsh, there is no doubt that the breed was well known to him:

"The Pomeranian or Wolf-dog.

The dog so called in this country is but a little more than eighteen or twenty inches in height and is distinguished by his long, thick, and rather upright coat, forming a most tremendous ruff about the neck, but short and smooth on the head and ears; they are mostly of a pale yellow, or cream-colour, and lightest on the lower parts. Some are white, some few black, and others but rarely spotted; the head broad towards the neck,

19.1 Pomeranian. Ch. Cygal's Baby Love.
Photo: Fall.

19.2 Pomeranian. Ch. Golden Star of Hadleigh.
Photo: Fall.

and narrowing to the muzzle; ears short, pointed and erect; nose and eyes mostly black; the tail large and bushy, invariably curled in a ring upon the back. Instances of smooth or short-coated ones are very rarely seen; in England he is much more familarly known by the name of fox-dog, and this may have originally preceeded from his bearing much more affinity to that animal about the head; but, by those who in their writings describe him as a native of Pomerania, he passes under the appellation of the Pomeranian-dog.

In general opinion, as a house-dog, he is held but in slender estimation, being by nature frivolous, artful, noisy, quarrelsome, cowardly, petulant, and deceitful, snappish and dangerous to children, without one predominant property of perfection to recommend him. This breed of dogs are common in Holland and have been occasionally introduced as a heiroglyphic by the caricaturist partizans of the House of Orange (in opposition to the Pug) to ridicule the patriots in their political disputes. There is this peculiarity in the coat of this dog, his hair, particularly the ruff about his neck, is not formed of hairs calculated to form the serpentine, or line of beauty, but is simply a semi-circle, which, by inclining the same way in large masses, give him a respectable and attractive appearance;; and, although they do not betray so great a degree of fondness and affection for their owners as some others of the species, yet they are not to be readily, or easily seduced. The largest of these dogs are used for draught in different countries, and it may, with well founded reason, be presumed, that to these, or a race somewhat similar, be attributed to Tooke's dogs in his *View of the Russian Empire*."

Taplin gave considerable space to describing the role of the larger draught-type dogs including the Samoyed and the Spitz type to be found in almost all the nomadic nations and tribes. Mr. Hicks also linked the Pomeranian with these, drawing particular attention to the characteristic tail carriage of the Spitz breeds.

In his book *Siberia in Europe* Henry Seebohm says of the Samoyed:

"The dogs were all white, except one, which was quite black. They were stiff-built little animals, somewhat like Pomeranian dogs, with fox-like head, and thick busy hair; their tails turned up over their back, and curled to one side. This similarity between the Pomeranian and Samoyede dogs is a rather curious fact, for Erman mentions a race of people, who, he says, resemble the Finns, both in language and features, in a district of Pomerania called Samogitia, inhabited by Samaites."

Mr. Hicks regards this statement as very important to those interested in the origin of the Pomeranian. At the beginning of this century they were pure white, and although not in a position to prove it, he feels sure that the breed is descended from the Samoyed. One of the most famous breeders of this dog was Mrs. Kilburn Scott and referring to the size of her dogs she said:

"We have bred Samoyedes for over twelve years and find that unless constantly importing fresh blood, our Samoyedes grow smaller."

A different point of view was expressed by a German judge and published in a Stuttgart newspaper in 1898. Herr Albert Kull said:

"Instead of speaking of breeds of German dogs I should be amply justified in calling them Wurtemburg breeds, for there is no denying the fact that the best specimens of Bull-dogs, Leonburgs, Poodles, Pomeranians and Dachshunds have been obtained from Wurtemburg as early as the fifties, and are still partly obtained from there to-day. The breeding and knowledge of dogs which is now in such a flourishing state in Germany, originated in Wurtemburg ... Wurtemburg dealers and breeders were the first to obtain due recognition for home-bred dogs at the Exhibitions of London, Paris and Vienna. Numerous fine specimens were thence exported to all parts of Germany, Austria and Switzerland."

Mr. Hicks said that in fairness he presented this opinion from a German expert, but it did not alter his own view that the breed was descended from some arctic race (probably the Samoyed) and brought into Pomerania at a very early period of the migration of the Samoyed tribes into the Samogitia region. It is of course accepted that the Pomeranian was at some time introduced into Germany and Austria and the rest of Europe, usually under a different name in each - Spitz, Wolfspitz, Volpino, Lupino, Lulu, Pommer and Pomeranian.

Since those days the Pomeranian has changed almost beyond recognition. In 1871 at a show judged by a great personality, Mr. William Lort, there were three entries, but the following year this had risen to thirteen under Mr. S. Handley. The numbers fluctuated but it was not until 1893 that entries had risen to over twenty when five classes were scheduled and judged by Mr. Frederick Gresham. The first prize winners were Mrs. Thomas's four dogs, *Black Boy, King Pippin, Pretty Boy II, Queen Bee*, and Miss C.A.D. Hamilton's *Rob of Rozelle*. There were twelve exhibitors and this was the turning point. Within three years forty to sixty entries were common and the number of classes had trebled. By the turn of the century entries of over 100 were usual and in 1905 at the Jubilee show of the Kennel Club the breed topped the entry with one hundred and twenty-five dogs. Mr. Hicks said that the question naturally arose - to what cause was this sudden and lasting change in the direction of our breed? It was, he says, due to the formation of the Pomeranian Dog Club which was registered at the Kennel Club on 7th August, 1894.

In 1901 the wording of the breed *standard* was studied and a few alterations made. One was in regard to the ears and it was expressly stated that "no plucking or trimming is allowed" and concerning the legs "no trimming is allowed". In 1896 a special resolution made the subject of trimming very clear "Every Pomeranian exhibited must be shown in a natural state, and that no clipping or plucking of the hair on the ears or face or feet or anywhere be countenanced or allowed." Obviously this was difficult to enforce as the matter came forward again nine years later when it was decided that the rule must be continued. The Pomeranian must have been at the height of its popularity then as the leading toy breed until it relinquished that position to the Pekingese.

The connection of the Pomeranian with our Royal Family is interesting. Queen Victoria had many pets and the usual story quoted is about her spaniel, *Dash*. However, she was very devoted to her Pomeranians and two very special dogs which she had until she died in 1901 were *Marco*, described as brown, whose face was getting white with age and *Turi*, a lovely little white dog. These two dogs had their portraits painted in 1900 by the well known miniaturist, Gertrude Massey, commissioned by the Prince and Princess of Wales as their last gift to her.

There is a wide variety of colour in this breed, and the breed *standard* is very detailed on this point, but for the pet it is entirely a matter of preference.

The old rules against trimming having long since been abandoned, the show Pomeranian needs careful preparation and trimming. Otherwise daily grooming will keep him in good condition.

Dr. Gordon Stables, who probably knew as much about dogs as any man of his generation, said some fifty years ago that the Pomeranian:

"has a great many good qualities to recommend him. He is very obedient, very tractable and teachable. He can be taught nearly as many tricks as a Poodle, and to receive and carry into the bargain. Moreover, he is an excellent guard to property, and if he cannot fight he can at all events give warning ... The Pomeranian is extremely affectionate towards those he really likes, and will remain faithful to the death. Some people will tell you that the dog is apt to be uncertain in temper. To strangers he may be at times, although even of this I have my doubts ... It is so easy to take away a dog's character."

Like other very small dogs, weighing between four and five and a half pounds, it is unwise to embark upon breeding without first acquiring some knowledge from an experienced breeder.

We should mention that sometimes the Pomeranian can be noisy in his desire to take his place as the house-dog, but with good training as a puppy it is easy to correct him.

This little dog makes a lively small pet, attractive and dainty. It is also an asset that he is so easy to pick up if necessary, and he certainly receives a lot of admiration from everyone.

19.3 An early Pomeranian. (From a cigarette card, 1924).

19.4 Pet Pomeranians (1930).

*19.5 Pomeranian. Ch. Ringlands Forest Fire of Quevain.
Owned by Mr. & Mrs. J. Watkins.*
Photo: Pearce.

Chapter 20

PUG

There is considerable difference of opinion about the origin of this most interesting breed. Some authorities are certain it came to Europe from China whilst others are equally certain it is of European derivation. Some suggest a possible source is Russia or even the British Isles, the suggestion being it was perhaps a bantamised Mastiff.

James Watson in *The Dog Book* (1906) considered that the Pug, in his peculiarities had no counterpart in any European breed but was likely to have originated in China. There is a strong resemblance between the Pug, the smooth coated so-called Pekingese Pug and the Chinese Happa dog, and we find that opinion convincing.

Although many Pugs came to the United Kingdom from Holland we have also to remember that one of the most famous of all Pugs who did so much to improve the breed was *Click*, described as an apricot- fawn, sired by *Lamb* (from Pekin) ex *Moss*. There was some doubt about *Moss's* nationality as she was not listed in the first Kennel Club stud book of 1874 as imported, but we cannot feel this is evidence that she was not bred in China. In those early days facts were often difficult to obtain for the stud book. Both *Moss* and *Lamb* were said by Mr. R. F. Mayhew, whose mother owned *Click*, to have been Chinese beyond dispute, captured in the Imperial Palace during the seige of Pekin in 1867 or 1868 and brought to the United Kingdom.

Although we are not going to delve more closely into the origin of the breed, one fact is informative, that is the name of "pug". The word was

20.1 Pug. Ch. Nanchyl Xerxes.
Photo: Marc Henrie, ASC.

not always associated with a breed of dog; several definitions can be found: *Sheridan's Dictionary*, 1780 says:

"Pug. f. A kind name of monkey, or anything tenderly loved."

Much earlier is the well known quotation - J. Crull, 1698:

"The monkey by chance came jumping out with them ... Poor pug was had before his betters."

Johnson's Dictionary defines "Pug" as puck, an imp or fairy, and Ada Milner in *Les Chiens d'Agrément* (1924) explains more fully:

"A form of Puck, the fairy or hobgoblin; applied to a dog it means a goblinlike creature. A dwarf variety of dog; a small dog which bears a miniature resemblance to a Bulldog."

Whilst Roget's *Thesaurus of English Words and Phrases* gives as an alternative meaning for "pug": stumpy, thickset or stocky.

There seems to be no reliable record of Pug dogs before the reign of William III (1688-1702) when they were introduced from Holland. According to legend, William the Silent escaped from a raid on his camp during the war with the Spaniards because his pet Pug raised the alarm. His gratitude ensured that for ever after the Royal House of Holland was never without Pugs.

The famous painter, William Hogarth, was devoted to the breed. In consequence he seems to have suffered a great deal of ridicule and was subject to the venom of his fellow caricaturists. His great pet and companion, the Pug *Trump* was with him in a self-portrait which can now be seen in the Tate Gallery, London. He also painted a picture of a black Pug in 1730 with the children of the first Earl of Pomfret. The French sculptor, Roubiliac, who was a friend of Hogarth and completed a bust of the painter which is in the National Portrait Gallery, London, also modelled *Trump*. Lap dogs were fashionable at this time and continued to flourish for a number of years. No lady of fashion was seen without her Pug dog and her black page boy.

In 1807 Thomas Bewick says of the Pug Dog:

"In outward appearance, in every way formed like the Bull-dog: but much smaller, and its tail is curled upon its back. It was formerly very common in many parts of England; however, at present, it is rarely to be met with."

By 1859 the Pug was slowly regaining popularity, according to "Stonehenge" in *The Dog in Health & Disease* (1867), but thirteen years later H. R. Richardson feared that the breed would soon become extinct, and "Idstone" *The Dog* (1872) bemoaned the lack of good specimens, saying:

"It would be hard to find more than half a dozen specimens equal to what existed a hundred years ago."

He said that one of the best he had ever seen was exhibited by Mr. Gurney of the Royal Exchange at the Maidstone Show of 1869.

Two years later proof of the renewed popularity of the Pug is confirmed by the entry at the Grand National Exhibition of Sporting and Other Dogs at the Crystal Palace, London held from 9th to 12th June 1874. Eight toy breeds were scheduled and judged by Messrs. J. Percival and S. Handley. The entry of Pugs totalled 48, and only one of them with cropped ears, a barbarous custom which was to be completely banned by the end of the century. Maltese had the next highest entry of 24. It was reported in the *Fancier's Gazette* of 18th June 1874 that the Pug entry was "the most numerous ever seen".

There has been controversy about the black Pug. Mrs. Swainston-Goodger in *The Pug Dog* (1930) says that she had never heard of any black specimens bred in this country before Lady Brassey's voyage but she had little doubt that many of the Russian and Chinese imports had black ancestors, as they were known in both countries. There could have been black Pugs in this country before those introduced by Lady Brassey when she returned from her voyage in the "Sunbeam" bringing with her *Mahdi* and *Jack Spratt*. Lady Brassey's account of that voyage, her visit to China and the dogs she saw is interesting reading in *Voyage of the "Sunbeam"*. Black Pugs were subsequently exhibited at the Maidstone show, all being from Lady Brassey's kennel, but it was not until 4th February 1896 that the Kennel Club granted separate classes for the black variety.

Pug owners are warm in their praise for the breed. He is said to be extremely fond of children and has considerable charm, making the perfect companion. He is not a fighter and will rarely attack anyone, but his deep toned bark makes him an excellent house dog. It is suggested that the fawns are more placid in temperament than the energetic blacks, but obviously this must depend to a large extent upon each individual dog.

His smooth coat makes him easier to keep in fine condition than some of the other toy breeds. Although daily grooming with a medium soft bristle brush is ideal, a day or two missed will not matter greatly. If desired, a coat conditioner spray can be used before brushing but it is important not to use it near his eyes. It is also unwise to brush the head as the bristles can so easily injure his rather prominent eyes, so a soft cloth or damped cotton wool is useful and will also keep the folds in the wrinkles clean. For the coat use a damp sponge or aerosol foam shampoo, apply carefully to the body and dry with a towel. It is customary to go over the dog at least once a week for any small injury or sign of parasites and to clean the teeth of an adult dog daily. A bath is seldom required if the dog is always well kept.

One of the principal works of fiction on this breed is *Three Curly Tails and others* (1909) by Marion Lockhart, written in aid of the poor children of Plaistow, East London. The nine full page coloured illustrations by W. Dacres Adams show five of *Mr. Puggers*, a black Pug with a red collar, and others of a Cocker Spaniel, a Deerhound and a Dandie Dinmont called *Dickie*. Arther Ransome sometimes included a Pug, *William*, in his stories of the Norfolk Broads.

20.2 A very early postcard of a Pug and her puppies (c.1904)

20.3 Pug. "The Pug" c.1913.

Chapter 21

YORKSHIRE TERRIER

This little terrier is truly British and is described in 1878 by Mr. Hugh Dalziel writing in Stonehenge's *Dogs of the British Islands* as:

"the newest goods of this class from the Yorkshire looms"

Even so, its origins, although not so uncertain as most of the toy dogs, show uncertainty about the varieties used in making this beautiful dog.

That it originated in Yorkshire is undoubtedly correct. Towns given credit for the manufacture of the Yorkshire Terrier are Bradford, Halifax, Huddersfield and Leeds. It was the pride and joy of the weavers and was said to be "the working man's dog". It was certainly a source of intense pleasure, treasured with great care by the wives of the workers who must have been responsible to a great extent for the beauty of the long flowing coat and the condition in which these dogs were kept.

The most probable foundation of the Yorkshire Terrier was the prick-eared Clydesdale. This breed was sometimes referred to as the Paisley Terrier, which, apart from his silky coat, resembled the Skye Terrier. The Clydesdale could have been crossed with the Miniature Black and Tan, later renamed the English Toy Terrier. Other breeds mentioned which may have been used were the Maltese, in our opinion probably less likely, and the Waterside Terrier - the dog which we know today as the Airedale. Mr. Reginald Knight, a reputable breeder, writing in Vero Shaw's *Illustrated Book of the Dog* (1881) says of the Waterside Terrier:

"This breed was originally bred from a cross between one of the old rough-coated Scotch Terriers and Bull Terrier...."

21.1 Yorkshire Terrier. Ch. Ozmilion Admiration.
Photo: Fall.

He continues with a list of suggested crossings which produced the Yorkshire Terrier through the Waterside Terrier, but the breeds suggested do not bear any resemblance to the Yorkshire Terrier and it is difficult to believe that such a mixture of types could have produced this little dog whose resemblance to the Clydesdale is so marked.

At the same time stressing that Bradford was the Yorkshire Terrier's earliest home, Mr. Robert Leighton tells us in *The Complete Book of the Dog* (1922) that the actual "inventor" of this breed was Mr. Peter Eden of Salford, Manchester, whom he describes as one of the earliest breeders and owners, reputed to have had a very charming breed of blue-tan terriers. Mr. Eden bought his early stock from Lancashire and although he may have given the new breed its first impulse it seems unlikely that it amounted to more than this.

There is however no doubt that the principal pioneers were Mr. and Mrs. Jonas Foster of Bradford who had previously shown other toy dogs, amongst these being the Maltese (then called the Maltese Terrier), Italian Greyhounds, Miniature Black and Tans (later English Toy Terriers), Toy Spaniels and Pugs. One of Mrs. Foster's dogs which was perhaps the most famous was *Huddersfield Ben*, bred by Mr. W. Eastwood of Huddersfield in 1865. During his short life - he was run over and killed in September 1871 - he won numerous prizes and was used at stud. Mrs. Foster considered he was responsible for many of her top winners.

Another particularly famous dog of hers was Ch. *Ted* (a grandson of *Huddersfield Ben*) who was considered the "flower of the flock" and won over two hundred prizes.

Mr. and Mrs. Foster were known throughout the world of show dogs and were even photographed and interviewed for a well known American publication on dogs. It is said that Mrs. Foster caused a sensation when she judged at the Manchester Dog Show held at St. James Hall from 26th to 28th March 1889. She was probably the first lady to officiate at so important a show and said she enjoyed this unique position. She had sufficient courage of her opinions to enter the ring and make the awards before a critical public. It was the second show of a new series and drew an "enormous" total of nearly 1,600 dogs. Her comment in the Kennel Gazette of April 1889 was:

"Schipperkes. Were put down for me to judge. I was not aware of it until I reached the show, and not being a keeper, breeder or exhibitor of these dogs, selected those that suited my fancy best ..."

It appears, however, that this distinction was also claimed by Miss M. A. E. Holdsworth who was appointed to judge her own breed, Pugs, at

Maidstone in 1886 but it is not certain whether or not this was comparable to the large northern show.

Mrs. Raymond-Mallock, well known in many toy breeds earlier this century, spoke very highly of Mrs. Foster and her dogs. Shortly before her death Mrs. Foster gave Mrs. Raymond-Mallock a photograph of *Huddersfield Ben*. To her great regret she lost it. This was indeed a pity as almost all the pictures we have seen of the dog were taken after the expert handling of the taxidermist, and however well done the result can never be quite the same. Mrs. Raymond-Mallock also said that on the back of the photograph was a list of *Ben's* winnings, a valuable record.

The Yorkshire Terrier was one of the first breeds to be registered at the Kennel Club founded by Mr. S. E. Shirley of Ettington in 1873, and the breed was entered in the first Stud Book published in 1874. This was edited by Mr. Frank C. S. Pearce, son of the Rev. Thomas Pearce, well known as "Idstone" of *The Field* and author of *The Dog* (1872).

The Yorkshire Terrier is a gay, happy little dog with the sporting character of a terrier. He enjoys a walk, particularly in the country in common with most terriers. He is alert, a good housedog and an ideal companion. If he is not required for show it is best to keep his silky coat to a reasonable length and to prevent tangles brush him daily. If desired the long hair on his head can be gathered and tied up with a red bow, or if preferred it may be left loose. It is easy to keep him tidy if his body coat is not allowed to grow too long, but if he is required for show then a great deal of care is necessary to keep him in the immaculate condition required. Recommended size is up to seven pounds in weight, which is sensible for a dog required as a pet.

Always make sure he has no tangles before bathing him, and every day see that his mouth and whiskers are clean and free from any dirt or food particles. Teeth should be kept clean and food given as dry as possible. As a young dog he should be able to eat puppy biscuit dry which will help to clean and preserve his teeth.

An interesting and authentic story of a Yorkshire Terrier is told by Mrs. Aileen M. Martello in *The Yorkshire Terrier* (1971). This is of course exceptional, but it does give some indication of the character of this small breed. To quote from the book:

"*Corporal Smoky* was the most famous and most decorated American-owned mascot in the Pacific and Asiatic areas during World War II."

In February 1944 she was found in an abandoned Japanese foxhole in the jungle, near Nadzab, New Guinea. She weighed less than four pounds and was about a year old. She became a member of a photo reconnaisance squadron of the Air Force. Her owner, Corporal Wynne, was an excellent trainer and Smoky was an exceptionally bright pupil. She learnt many tricks and entertained hundreds of service men in hospitals in Australia, New Guinea and the Phillipines during two years of active service. Her blanket was made of green felt from a card table. On this coat she wore the Fifth Air Force badge and a WAC ribbon. Her tricks were numerous and on one memorable occasion she pulled a telegraph wire through an 8-inch pipe for a distance of 70 feet under an air strip, saving the signal corps many hours of digging.

On retirement she and her owner travelled all over the United States and performed before an estimated six million people. In 1954 they had their own thirty week television show on "How to Train your dog".

Corporal Smoky was buried on 21 January, 1957. Nobody ever discovered who her original owner was or anything of her background before she was found in the foxhole.

There are several works of fiction on the breed, one of the oldest being M. Montgomery-Campbell's *The Chronicles of Baba*, an authentic and interesting story with excellent old photographs, published in 1901. Robert Nathan's several stories about *Tapiola*, the Yorkshire Terrier, are also popular and so is R. Callender's *I'm Nick*, published in 1938.

21.2 Yorkshire Terrier. Ch. Ozmilion Dedication.
Photo: Fall.

21.3 Yorkshire Terrier. Ch. Yadnum Regal Fare.
Owned by Miss Vera Munday.
Photo: Sally Anne Thompson

SUMMARY

This concludes our brief history of the toy breeds, their characters and temperaments. We hope the book is of use to those anxious to find a suitable companion toy dog. With so many breeds from which to choose it should not be difficult to find one to fit ideally into the household.

From the flat nose varieties one has the choice of the long coated King Charles Spaniel, the Pekingese or the Japanese Chin; from the smooth coated variety the Pug, and the Griffon Bruxellois, which can be smooth or rough.

The Terrier varieties include the smooth coated English Toy Terrier or the Miniature Pinscher. The Yorkshire Terrier has a long coat which requires constant care. the much rarer Australian Silky Terrier has a slightly shorter coat and the Affenpinscher is rough coated.

The Spaniel types include the very popular Cavalier King Charles Spaniel and the dainty Papillon, all of whose coats need regular attention.

There is also the minute Chihuahua, which can be either long or smooth coated; the breed which resembles a lion, the Lowchen; the unusual hairless dog, the Chinese Crested; the elegant and stylish Italian Greyhound, the white coated Bichon Frisé and the Maltese, who both need regular grooming, and the lively and confident Pomeranian.

These breeds offer a wide variety of choice to suit everyone's requirements.

The amount of general care required is similar in all breeds but there are variations for each and every one. We remind the reader again that specific books are available on the detailed care and management for each individual breed.

We also recommend the reader to seek further advice and information before reaching a decision on selecting a breed.

Showing and breeding are not within the scope of this book. If it is intended to enter into these activities then a great deal more knowledge of the chosen breed is necessary before even making the initial purchase. In addition it is wise to study the current breed *standard* which is contained in a booklet, *Breed Standards - Toy Group No. 6.* published by and obtainable from The Kennel Club, 1, Clarges Street, Piccadilly, London, W1Y 8AB.

The Kennel Club will also supply the name and address of the current secretary of the breed club who will be able to recommend a breeder. Do not be surprised if these people ask for particulars of the household and conditions prevailing. Good breeders are very conscious of their responsibility for the future welfare of all the puppies they sell and will want to feel satisfied that the home offered is a suitable and permanent one. Pet shops and dealers can often supply puppies but their attitude is not always the same as that of the caring experienced breeder.

All toy dogs make delightful house pets, bring a lot of enjoyment to their owners and enrich their lives. Like all dogs they become very much a part of the family and a treasured possession.

SELECTED BIBLIOGRAPHY

Details of general books on toy dogs are listed below before those on individual breeds. All books are illustrated unless otherwise stated. Date of publication, usually of the first edition, is given after the name of the publisher.

American Kennel Club *Toy Dogs.*
The breeds and standards as recognised by the American Kennel Club. 99pp. G. Howard Watt, New York. 1935

Barton, Frank T. MRCVS. *Toy Dogs.*
Their points and management in health and disease. 210 pp. R. A. Everett & Co. London. 1904
Toy Dogs. New and enlarged edition. 1913
My Book of Little Dogs. 106 pp. Illustrated by G. Vernon Stokes. Jarrold & Sons, London. 1911

Bouctot-Vagniez, Mme. *Les Chiens d'Agrément et la SFACA.*
79pp. Toy Dogs recognised by the Fédération Cynologique Internationale. 125 copies printed. Le Vestinet, editions Sport Canin. France. C 1938. In French.

Collier, V.W.F. *Dogs of China and Japan in Nature and Art.*
207 pp. William Heinemann, London. 1921

Foreman, Mrs. R.A. *Small Dog Obedience Training.*
170pp. Nimrod Press, Alton, Hants, United Kingdom. 1987

Dangerfield, Stanley *Dogs: Toy and Miniature Breeds.*
151 pp. Arco Pet Library, New York. 1967

Diehl, John E.   *The Toy Dog.*
   82 pp. Associated Fanciers, Philadelphia. U.S.A. 1899

Glover, Harry   *Toy Dogs.*
   110 pp. Illustrated with photographs and drawings by the author.
David & Charles, Newton Abbot, United Kingdom. 1977

Kalstone, Shirlee   *The Kalstone Guide to Grooming all Toy Dogs.*
   176 pp. Photographs by Larry Kalstone, drawings by Vivian Falzetti.
Howell Book House Inc., New York. 1976

Legl-Jacobsson, Elisabeth   *East Asiatic Breeds.*
   277 pp. Tryck Produktions, Sweden. 1978

Leighton, George   *Home Treatment of Dogs.*
   Toys and others. 47 pp. George Bell & Sons, London. 1905

Lytton, The Hon. Mrs. Neville   *Toy Dogs and their Ancestors.*
   Including the history and management of Toy Spaniels, Pekingese,
Japanese and Pomeranians. 359 pp. Duckworth, London. 1911

Toy Dogs and their Ancestors.
   D. Appleton & Co, New York. 1911

Maxtee, John   *Popular Toy Dogs.*
   Their breeding, exhibition and management. 127 pp. The Bazaar,
Exchange & Mart, London. 1922

Popular Toy Dogs. 2nd Edition. c. 1930.

Megnin, Pierre   *Le Chien et ses Races.*
   3rd edition revised and enlarged. Short chapter on health by Henri
Benjamin. Vincennes, Paris. 1910. An earlier edition 1889-1891 was
published in three volumes. In French.

Milner, Mme. Ada   *Les Chiens d'Agrément.*
   234 pp. Illustrated with paintings by the author and photographs.
Section on maladies and treatment. Parallel French and English text.
Translated from the French by L. Martineau. Privately printed in
edition of 1120 copies in 1924. Paris.

Mockesch, Eduard   *Des Kleinhundebuch*
   (The Toy-dog book) Kosmos-Verlag. Germany. 1980. In German.

Raymond-Mallock, L.   *Toy Dogs.*
   The History, Points and Standards of Pekingese, Toy Spaniels,
Japanese, Pomeranians, Yorkshire and Toy Terriers, Schipperkes,
Pugs, Griffon Bruxellois, Maltese and Italian Greyhounds, with
instructive chapters on Breeding, Rearing, Feeding, Training and
Showing; and full information as to treatment of most ailments.

178pp. Privately printed C 1914. (Later editions published as The Up-to-Date Pekingese and all other Toy Dogs). United Kingdom.

The Up-to-date Pekingese and all other Toy Dogs. 4th edition. The above breeds with the addition of the Papillon. 339 ppp. Privately printed C 1925. United Kingdom.

Ricketts, Viva Leone   *All About Toy Dogs.*
Their care in Sickness and Health. Feeding, Training, Breeding and the History and Character of each breed. 200 pp. Howell Book House Inc. New York 1965, and Robert Hale, London. 1969.

Rine, Josephine Z.   *Toy Dogs.*
Their History, Care and Management. 187 pp. Orange Judd Publshing Co., New York. 1933

Sheldon, Margaret, and Lockwood, Barbara   *The Toy Breeds.*
121 pp. Pelham Books, London. 1970.

Sigfridsson, Lisbeth   *Dvarg Hund Boken.*
NYA forlaget, Sweden. In Swedish.

Williams, Mrs. Leslie   *A Manual of Toy Dogs and their treatment.*
How to Feed, Rear and Breed them. 106 pp. Edward Arnold, London. 1910 and later editions.

The Puppy Manual. A guide to rearing puppies from birth to maturity, with a chapter on buying and selling puppies. 61 pp. 2nd edition 1906. Dog World, Idle, Bradford, United Kingdom.

Wimhurst, C.G.E.   *The Book of Toy Dogs.*
207 pp. Frederick Muller, London. 1965.

Magazine:

National Geographic Magazine April 1944. U.S.A.Special feature: *Freeman Lloyd on Toy Dogs, Pets of Kings and Commoners.* Pages 459-472.

Affenpinscher

Affenpinscher Club of America, Inc.   *To introduce the breed*
- a 12 page pamphlet in typescript and with one picture.

Gibbs, D.V. and Tobin, Jackson   *How to raise and Train an*
                                                        Affenpinscher.
64 pp. T.F.H. Publications, New Jersey, U.S.A. 1969

Australian Silky Terrier

Hamilton-Wilkes, M.   *The Australian Silky Terrier.*
86 pp. Angus & Robertson, New South Wales, Australia. 1965.

Lehnig, Beverly   *Your Silky Terrier.*
    128 pp. Denlinger's, U.S.A. 1972.
Scott, O.R.   *The Australian Silky Terrier.*
    Lovable Silkies. Gold Medal Publications, New South Wales, Australia.
    1969.
Smith, Mrs. Merle E.   *American Kennel Club Silky Terrier Champions.*
    Pedigree volume. California, U.S.A. 1973.
Weil, Martin   *Silky Terriers.*
Wheatland, W.A. (Fred)   *The Australian Terrier and the Australian*
                                                Silky Terrier.
    58 pp. including glossary. 28 pages on the Silky. Swales & Co. PTY
    Limited, Mosman, New South Wales, Australia. 1964.
Young, Betty   *This is the Silky Terrier.*
    302 pp. T.F.H. Publications, New Jersey, U.S.A. 1972.
    How to Raise and Train a Silky Terrier.
    64 pp. T.F.H. Publications, New Jersey, U.S.A. 1963.

Bichon Frisé

Beauchamp, Dick   *The Bichon Frisé Handbook.*
    48 pp. Rohman Publications, California, U.S.A. 1972.
    The Bichon Frisé Workbook. 96 pp. Rohman Publications, California,
    U.S.A. 1975.
Beauchamp, Richard   *The Bichon Frisé Today.*
    200 pp. (Spiral bound) Rohman Publications, California, U.S.A. 1982.
Bichon Frisé Club of San Diego   *The Bichon Frisé: Twenty-five years.*
    276 pp. A pictorial Review. California, U.S.A. 1985.
Brearley, Joan M. *Nicholas, Anna K.*   *This is the Bichon Frisé.*
    320 pp. T.F.H. Publications, New Jersey, U.S.A.
Hutchison, John E.   *The Bichon Frisé..*
    A Practical Approach. 91 pp. Privately published. Australia. 1986.
Ransom, Jackie   *The Dog Directory Guide to the Bichon Frisé.*
    121 pp. Bracknell, United Kingdom. 1978.
Bichon Frisé Great Britain Pedigree Book.
    32 pp. Privately published. United Kingdom. 1985.
Weill, Martin   *Bichon Frisé..*
    125 pp. T.F.H. Publications, Hong Kong. 1981.

Cavalier King Charles Spaniel

Booth, Evelyn *All About the Cavalier King Charles Spaniel.*
174 pp. Pelham Books, London. 1983.

Burgess, S. *The Cavalier King Charles Spaniel.*
102 pp. K. R. Books, Edlington, Lincs, United Kingdom. 1975.

Forwood, Mary (Lady) *The Cavalier King Charles Spaniel.*
144 pp. Popular Dogs, London. 1967.

Kelley, Anne *Daisy and the Dog Show.*
16 pp. Illustrated by Metin Salih. Aurum Press, London. 1985.
Daisy's Discovery. 16pp. Illustrated by Metin Salih. Aurum Press, London. 1985.

McKenzie, Barbara *Your First Cavalier.*
126 pp. Press, Maldon, Essex, United Kingdom. 1985.

Spalding, Elizabeth C. *How to Raise and Train a Cavalier King Charles Spaniel.*
64 pp. T.F.H. Publications, New Jersey, U.S.A. 1965.

Stenning, Eilidh M. *Cavalier King Charles Spaniels.*
75 pp. W. & G. Foyle, London. 1964.

Stopford, Richard E. *The Cavalier Spaniel and its Derivations.*
16 pp. Arthur Stockwell Ltd, Ilfracombe, Devon, United Kingdom. 1951.

Chihuahua

Biala, Karin *Der Chihuahua.*
Kosmos-Verlag, Germany. 1985. In German.

Casselli, Rosina, et al. *The Complete Chihuahua.*
New revised 4th edition. 256 pp. of which 128 are on the breed. Remainder general care. Howell Book House Inc., New York. 1967.

Denlinger, Milo G. *The Complete Chihuahua, 2nd edition.*
224 pp. 96 of which are on the breed. Remainder general care. Denlinger's, U.S.A. 1950.

Dorrance, Gordon *A Dog's Tale, the true tale of little Chickie Chihuahua (herself).*
Edited by Emile Dorrance. 165 pp. Philadelphia, U.S.A. 1963.

Ferguson, Estelle Barbaresi, Sara M. *How to Raise and Train a Chihuahua.*
64 pp. T.F.H. Publications, New Jersey, U.S.A. 1958.

Garrett, Ida H.   *The Chihuahua.*
   31 pp. Louis Minsky, New York. 1933.

Gehring, Hugo   *Der Chihuahua.*
   Rudolf Muller, Koln, Germany. 1986. In German.

Gray, Thelma   *The Popular Chihuahua.*
   224 pp. Popular Dogs Publishing Company, London. 1961.
   The Chihuahua. 224 pp. Revised and re-printed. Popular Dogs
   Publishing Company, London. 1967.

Harmar, Hilary   *Chihuahuas.*
   120 pp. W. *G. Foyle, London. 1966.*
   Chihuahua Guide. 248 pp. Pet Library, New York. 1969.
   The Complete Chihuahua Encyclopaedia. 373 pp. John Bartholomew,
   United Kingdom. 1972.

Huxham, Mona   *All About Chihuahuas.*
   192 pp. Pelham Books, London. 1976.

Kauffman, Russell E.   *The Chihuahua.*
   A complete Presentation. 158 pp. of which 78 are on the breed.
   Remainder general cared. Judy Publishing Company, Chicago, U.S.A.
   1952.
   The Chihuahua. 2nd edition. 160 pp. equally divided between breed
   and general care. 1959.

"Mard" (M. Diana Russell Allen)   *Little Cupid.*
   41 pp. Illustrations by Beshlie Heron. Privately printed, n.d., United
   Kingdom.

Miller, madeline   *Chihuahua as Pets*:
   a guide to the selection, care and breeding. 32 pp. T.F.H. Publications,
   New Jersey, U.S.A. 1955.

Murray, Ruth L.   *Your Chihuahua.*
   128 pp. Hawthorn, New York. 1966.

Pisano, Beverley (Editor)   *Chihuahuas.*
   125 pp. T.F.H. Publications, Hong Kong. 1980.

Riddle, Maxwell   *This is the Chihuahua.*
   191 pp. T.F.H. Publications, New Jersey. U.S.A. 1959.

Schneider, Earl (Editor)   *Know your Chihuahua.*
   64 pp. Pet Library, New York.
   Enjoy your Chihuahua. 32 pp. Pet Library, New York.

Thurmer, Tressa E. & Gentile, F.L. DVM   *Pet Chihuahua.*
64 pp. All-Pets books Inc., fond du Lac, Wisconsin, U.S.A. 1954.

Townesend, Stephen FRCS   *A Thoroughbred Mongrel.*
1st edition. The Tale of a Dog told by a Dog to lovers of Dogs. 175 pp.
Illustrated by J.A. Shepherd (on the tital page J.A. Shepperd). T. Fisher
Unwin, London. 1900.

A Thoroughbred Mongrel. 8th edition. Includes "HETT" an
appreciation. 188 pp. 1913.

Wall, Charles H.   *This and That about Chihuahuas.*
98 pp. 2nd edition. Buddy Publishing Company, Toronto, Canada.
1950.

This and That about Chihuahuas. 124 pp. 3rd edition revised and
enlarged. Buddy Publishing Company, Toronto, Canada. 1956.

Chinese Crested Dog

Cardew, Mirri   *A Chinese Crested for me.*
48 pp. Midland Counties Publications, Earl Shilton, United Kingdom.
1986.

Gorwill, Sylvia. G.   *The Hairless Dogs of the World.*
71 pp. Privately printed 1987. United Kingdom.

Van der Lyn, Edita   *How to Raise and Train a Chinese Crested.*
64 pp. T.F.H. Publications, New Jersey, U.S.A. 1964.

English Toy Terrier (Black and Tan)

Clark, Russell D.   *Russell's Famous Strain, Toy Manchester Terriers.*
Gen, Virginia, U.S.A. 1937.

Dempsey, Dixie   *The Complete Toy Manchester Terrier.*
256 pp. of which 114 are on the breed. Remainder general care.
Denlinger's, U.S.A. 1950.

Lamb, Lady   *The Veracious History of a Black and Tan Terrier.*
told by himself. 79pp. Newman, London. 1880.

Mack, Janet   *Pet Manchester.*
80pp. Includes English Toy Terrier and also "Your Manchester's
Health" by Dr. Nancy Riser. All-Pets books, Fond du Lac, Wisconsin,
U.S.A. 1958.

Miller, Evelyn   *Manchester Terriers.*
A Guide to the selection and breeding of Toy Manchesters. 26 pp.
T.F.H. Publications, New Jersey, U.S.A. 1957.

Simpson, Eve Blantye   *Nelson and Puck.*
   Dogs of other days. 111 pp. William blackwood, London. 1882.

Tracy, Julia Lowndes   *Terrier V.C.*
   46 pp. Aldine Publishing Company, London. C 1915.

Wortley, Isabel   *Topay's Four Homes and visits.*
   270 pp. Jarrold & Sons, London. C 1900.

Topsy's Travels and Adventures. London, 1905.

Youmans, Eleanor   *Cinder.*
   Story of a Black and Tan Terrier. 132 pp. Illustrated by F. Bernard
   Shields. Bobbs-Merrill, Indianapolis, U.S.A. 1933.

Griffon Bruxellois

Cousens, Marjorie   *Griffon Bruxellois.*
   106 pp. W. G. Foyle, London. 1960.

The Second Book of the Griffon Bruxellois. 86 pp. Frontis of the author.
Tables of lines and families. Privately printed. United Kingdom. 1969.

Parker-Rhodes, Mabel   *The Cult of the Griffon Bruxellois.*
   62 pp. Watmough Limited, Idle and London. 1926.

The Cult of the Griffon Bruxellois. 2nd edition. 91 pp. 1931.

Raynham, L.C. (Doone)   *The History and Management of the*
                                            Griffon Bruxellois.
   144 pp. Scan Books, Brighton, United Kingdom. 1985.

Spicer, Muriel Handley   *Toy dogs. How to Breed and Rear Them.*
   Being the Life of a Griffon Bruxellois. 148 pp. 8 plates. Adam and
   Charles Black, London. 1902.

Weiss, Seymour   *How to Raise and Train a Griffon Bruxellois.*
   64 pp. T.F.H. Publications, New Jersey, U.S.A. 1969.

Italian Greyhound

Barber, Lillian   *The Italian Greyhound Guide.*
   86 pp. Italian Greyhound Productions, Washington D.C., U.S.A. 1983.

Baxendale, Esther M.   *Fairy, the Autobiography of a Real Dog.*
   310 pp. 1907. Boston, U.S.A. (Re-issue of "Yours with all my Heart"
   Boston, U.S.A. 1904)

Incontri, Maria Luisa   *Il Piccolo Levriero Italiano.*
   121 pp. Sansoni, Florence, Italy. In Italian. 1956.

Lathrop, Dorothy   *The Dog in the Tapestry Garden*
   42 pp. Illustrated by the author. Macmillan & Co, New York. 1962.

Oliver, Annette   *Living with Italian Greyhounds.*
87 pp. Privately printed. United Kingdom. 1983.

Russo, Louis F.   *How to Raise and Train an Italian Greyhound.*
64 pp. T.F.H. Publications, New Jersey, U.S.A. 1964.

Sherrill, James R.   *Description of the Ethnic characteristics of the Small Italian Greyhound.*
14 pp. Privately printed. 1965.

Stewart, Robert W.   *Structure and Movement in Italian Greyhounds.*
C. 1974. U.S.A.

Tangye, R.   *The Story of Little Gyp.*
London. 1892.

Thring, E.D.   *The Italian Greyhound.*
24 pp. The Italian Greyhound Club, United Kingdom. n.d.

Worthing, Eileen M.   *Life and Legends of the Italian Greyhound.*
32 pp. Illustrated by Irene F. Riedel. Privately published. n.d.

Japanese Chin

Alexander, Mrs. Claude C.   *How to Raise and Train a Japanese Spaniel.*
64 pp. T.F.H. Publications, New Jersey, U.S.A. 1960.

Collier, V.W.F.   *Dogs of China and Japan in Nature and Art.*
(See General Toy Books)

Legl-Jacobsson, Elisabeth   *East Asiatic Breeds.*
Pages 226 to 263 deal exclusively with the Japanese Chin. Tryck Produktions, Sweden. 1978.
Japanese Chin. 72 pp. G.P.R. Produktions, Sweden. 1982. In Swedish.

Muller-Probster, Paula   *Der Vernehme Zimmerhund.*
Japan Chin, Peking Palasthund, Toy Spaniel. 114 pp. Nurnberg, Germany. 1929. In German.

Schenck, Vera E.   *Japanese Spaniels as Pets.*
1 pp. T.F.H. Publications, New Jersey, U.S.A. 1960.

King Charles Spaniel

Birchall, M. Joyce   *King Charles Spaniels.*
77 pp. W. & G. Foyle, Lndon. 1960.

Gristwood, M.E.   *King Charles Spaniel Shispers.*
21 pp. Privately published. United Kingdom. 1983.

Hauer, Odd   *My Friend King Charles.*
32 pp. Privately printed. Hovik, Norway. 1953.

Muller-Probster, Paula *Der Vernehme Zimmerhund.*
Japan Chin, Pekin, Palasthund, Toy Spaniel. 114 pp. Nurnberg, Germany. Druk: Chr. Moser. 1929. In German.

Oyler, Leslie M. *Jock, Jill and Ginger.*
Illustrated by Ethel L. Tanner. Gale and Polden, London.

Paine, Mrs. Milton J. *How to Raise and Train a King Charles Spaniel.*
64 pp. T.F.H. Publications, New Jersey, U.S.A. 1964.

Umluff, Gerda M. *Die Zwergspaniels.*
80 pp. King Charles spaniels and Papillons. Albrecht Philler, Minden, Germany. 1979. In German.

Ward, Marcus *Dogs: Marcus Ward's Picture Book of Animals.*
16 pp. Mainly King Charles Spaniels. Marcus Ward, London. C 1870.

Maltese

Berndt, Robert J. *Your Maltese.*
128 pp. Denlinger's, U.S.A. 1975.

Brearley, Joan M. *The book of the Maltese.*
288 pp. T.F.H. Publications, New Jersey, U.S.A.

Cutillo, N. *The Complete Maltese.*
351 pp. Howell Book House Inc., New York. 1986.

Greaves, Lady (Millicent Josephine) *Me and Dod.*
158 pp. Herbert Jenkins, London. 1924.

Howell, Partricia M. *The Modern Maltese.*
Pollyanna Press Publications, Minnesota, U.S.A. 1967.

Iveria, Miki *Maltese Dogs.*
The Jewels of Women. 128 pp. The Maltese Club of Great britain. 1979.

Hunter, Mrs. C.M. *The Maltese.*
11 page leaflet. Hereford Times, C. 1950. United Kingdom.

Leitch, Virginia T. *The Maltese Dog.*
A History of the Breed. 458 pp. Privately printed. John Vir Kennels, Riversdale, Maryland, U.S.A. 1953.

Leitch, Virginia T./Carno, Dennis *The Maltese Dog.*
2nd revised edition. 490 pp. International Institute of Veterinary Science, New York. 1970.

Liebers, Arthur *How to Raise and Train a Maltese.*
64 pp. T.F.H. Publications, New Jersey, U.S.A. 1962.

Miller, Evelyn   *Maltese as pets.*
    T.F.H. Publications, New Jersey, U.S.A. 1961.
Nicholas, Anna K.   *The Maltese.*
    284 pp. T.F.H. Publications, New Jersey, U.S.A. 1984.
Schneider, Earl (Editor)   *Know your Maltese.*
    64 pp. Pet Library, New York.
Stuber, Marge   *I love Maltese.*
    62 pp. Privately published. Ohio, U.S.A. 1971.
    Breeding Toy Dogs .. especially Maltese.
    68 pp. Privately published. Ohio, U.S.A. 1976.

Article:

Ezzy, Mrs. E.V.   *The Maltese.*
    Published in The Toy Dog Club of Queensland Newsletter, Christmas
    1968. Australia.

Miniature Pinscher

Bagshaw, Margaret R.   *Pet Miniature Pinscher.*
    64 pp. Illustrated by Morgan Dennis. All-Pets Inc. Fond du Lac,
    Wisconsin, U.S.A. 1958.
Boshell, Boris, M.D.   *Your Miniature Pinscher.*
    160 pp. Denlinger's, U.S.A. 1969
Jones, Chips   *The Miniature Pinscher you may know.*
    Lund Press, Wisconsin, U.S.A. 1969.
Krogh, David M. & Sharon A.   *Miniature Pinschers in America.*
    A Comprehensive Record from 1970 - 1980. 190 pp. Privately printed,
    U.S.A. 1980.
Miller, Evelyn   *How to Raise and Train a Miniature Pinscher.*
    64 pp. T.F.H. Publications, New Jersey, U.S.A. 1961.
Miller, Madeline   *Miniature Pinschers.*
    A Guide to the selection care and breeding of Miniature Pinschers. 25
    pp. T.F.H. Publications, New Jersey, U.S.A. 1958.
Ricketts, Viva Leone   *The Complete Miniature Pinscher.*
    287 pp of which 159 are on the breed. Remainder general care. Details
    of the breed in other countries. Howell Book House Inc. New York.
    1972.

Papillon

Avebury, Diana, Lady   *Zelda and the Corgis.*
    56 pp. Illustrated by Sir Hugh Casson. Piccadilly Press, London. 1984.

Bolt, Erika — *Scchmetterlingshundchen: Papillon und Phalène.* 102 pp. Kynos-Verlag, Murlenbach. 1987. In German.

Bolt, Erika et al. — *Papillon/Phalène Rassesymposium Ludwigsburg.* 2nd May, 1981. 24 pp. In German.

Christensen, Runa — *Papillon.* 63pp. Clausen Boger, Copenhagen. 1975. In Danish.

de Rouck, R.G. — *Historique de la race Epagneul Nain Continental.* 69 pp. Ghent, Brussels. 1970. In French.

Gauss, D. Christian — *How to Raise and Train a Papillon.* 64 pp. T.F.H. Publications, New Jersey, U.S.A. 1964.

Knowles, Elizabeth — *Gertruude. By "Herself".* 24 pp. Illustrated by Peter Benson. Privately published. United Kingdom. 1974.

Houtart, Baron Albert — *Espagneuls Nains Continentaux.* 71 pp. Chasse et Pêche, Brussels. 1925. In French.

Millot, Dr. Albert — *L'Epagneul Nain Continental.* 49 pp. Privately printed Alfort, France. 1974. In French.

Radermacher, Mrs. — *The Papillon.* 10 pp. Privately printed. United Kingdom. 1955.

Russell Roberts, P. & B. — *The Papillon Handbook.* 134 pp. Nicholson Watson, London. 1959.

Sharwaany, Liz — *Papillon.* 68 pp. Clausen Boger, Copenhagen. 1987. In Danish.

Tamm, Suzanne — *Papillon och Phalène.* 96 pp. ICA Bokförlag, Vasteras, Sweden. 1978. In Swedish. *The Breed in Art.* Limited edition of 100 copies in Swedish and 50 each in French and English. Privately published. 1986/7.

Umlauff, Gerda M. — *Die Zwergspaniels.* King Charles and Papillons. 80pp. Albrecht Philler, Minden, Germany. 1979. In German.

Waud, Clarice & Hutchings, M.W. — *The Papillon 'Butterfly' Dog.* A Worldwide Comprehensive Study of the Breed. 300 pp. Nimrod Press, Alton, United Kingdom. 1985.

Waud, Clarice & Dowle, P. — *The Butterfly Dog (Papillon and Phalène).* 60 pp. Privately published, United Kingdom. 1976.

Waud, Clarice & Challis P. *The Butterfly Dog (Papillon Phalène)* 2nd edition revised and re-written. Nimrod Press, Alton, United Kingdom. 1986.

Pekingese

Allen, M. Loftus *Show Pekingese.* Origin; History; Standard of Points; How to breed, rear, treat and prepare for exhibition. 50 pp. Our Dogs Publishing Company, London. 1923.

Show pekingese. 2nd edition 1939.

Ash, Edward C. *The Pekingese as a Companion and Show dog.* Its care, management and history. Famous owners, breeders and dogs. 154 pp. Cassell, London. 1936.

Ashton Cross, Mrs. C. *The Pekingese Dog.* 369 pp. Privately published. United Kingdom. 1932.

Astley, H.D. *The Memoirs of No-Nosi.* 38 pp folio. Illustrated by the author. 50 copies only privately printed. United Kingdom. 1931.

Astley, L.P.C. Allen, Mrs. M. Loftus *The Perfect Pekingese. A Monograph.* 169 pp. Illustrated Kennel News, London. 1912.

Ayscough, F. *The Autobiography of a Chinese Dog.* 105 pp. Sketches by Lucille Douglass. Jonathan Cape, London. 1926.

Baker, Margaret *The Family that grew and grew.* 121 pp. Illustrated by Nora S.Unwin. London. 1962.

Batten, Joyce Mortimer *Chang.* The Life Story of a Pekingese. 103 pp. Illustrated by G. Vernon Stokes. Moray Press, Edinburgh. 1935.

Berndt, Robert J. *Your Pekingese.* Compiled and edited by William W. Denlinger and R. Annabel Rathman. 127 pp. Denlinger's, U.S.A. 1978.

Bland, J.O.P. and Backhouse, Sir E.T. *China under the Empress Dowager of China.* Eveleigh Nash. 1906.

Bondeli, Mme. la Baronne de *Le Pekinois.* Standard Historique. Paris C 1910. In French.

Bridge-Roberts, C.P. *A Peke's Tale.* 41 pp. Golden Pegasus Books, London. 1960.

Brown, Ivor   *Puck our Peke.*
    78 pp. George Routledge & Son, London. 1931.

"Camilla"   *Wee Jade Button*
    To the Pekingese Pom Pom. Much mourned companion of an alone
    child. Written and illustrated by the author (aged 16). Michael-Slains
    Publication, Switzerland. 1966.

Carl, Katherine A.   *With the Empress Dowager of China.*
    306 pp. The New Century Company, New York. 1906.

Chaya, Elenore   *The Little Lion Dog.*
    The smallest dog book in the world. 47 pp. No. 130 of Limited edition
    of 300 copies, printed by hand at the Borrowers Press, Cleveland
    Heights, Ohio, U.S.A. 1982.

Clarke,Pauline   *The Pekingese Princess.*
    143 pp. Illustrated by Cecil Leslie. Jonathan Cape, London. 1948.

Collier, V.W.F.   *Dogs of China and Japan in Nature and Art.*
    (See General Toy Books.)

Common Sense Remedy Co.   *The Pekingese Spaniel.*
    45 pp. New York. 1917.

Daly, Macdonald   *The Pekingese.*
    32 pp. Findon Publications, London. 1950.

Daniel M.N.   *Some Pekingese Pets.*
    75 pp Sektched and described by the author. John Lane, The Bodley
    Head, Kondon. 1914.

Davidson, George B. (Editor)   *The Pekingese Manual.*
    191 pp. The Lexicon Press, Calif. U.S.A. 1957.

Denlinger, Milo G.   *The Complete Pekingese.*
    280 pp. of which 168 are on the breed. Remainder general care.
    Denlinger's, U.S.A. 1949.

Dilssner, Hede   *Die Drei Pekingsen.*
    Berlin. 1935. In German.

Dixie, A. Coath   *The Lion Dog of Pekin.*
    Being the astonishing History of the Pekingese Dog. 245 pp. Peter
    Davis, London. 1931.
    The Lion Dog of Pekin. Revised edition. 1967.

Dorey, Benny Engel   *The Sleeve Dog.*
    125 pp. Thornhill press, Gloucester, U.S.A. 1975.
    Elsie Sho No Mi. Vantage Press, new York. 1969.

Drowne, T.B.   *But Charlie wasn't listening.*
30 pp. Illustrated by Helen Meredith. Pantheon Books, New York.
1960.

Dyer, Walter A.   *All Around Robin Hood's Barn.*
204 pp. william Heinemann, London. 1926.

Eldon, Magdalen   *Bumble.*
Illustrated by the author, Unpaged. Collins, London. 1950.
Snow bumble. ... Unpaged. 1951.
Highland Bumble. ... Unpaged. 1952.
Bumble and the Bunnies. ... Unpaged. 1953.

"Go Bang" (Isabel K. Benjamin)   *Letters from a Pekingese.*
Cover design by Maud Earl. Edwin S. Gorham, New York. 1920.

Godbold, Bridget   *Pekingese in Australia.*
155 pp. Jacaranda Press, Brisbane, Australia. 1962.
No Time for Sleeping. Illustrated by Madeline Brown. Brisbane,
Australia. 1983.

Godden, Rumer   *Chinese Puzzle.*
149 pp. Peter Davis, London. 1936.
The Butterfly Lions. The Pekingese in History, Legend and Art. 192 pp.
Macmillan, London. 1977.

Harman, Ian   *Pekingese.*
96 pp. Williams & Norgate, London. 1949.

Hempel, Patte   *Pekingese Profiles.*
43 pp. Illustrated by Tina Orcutt. Sprial binding. San Jose Barking
Dogs, U.S.A. 1985.

Hill, H. Warner   *Pekingese.*
78 pp. W. & G. Foyle, London. 1957.

Hogner, Dorothy   *Little Esther.*
63 pp. Illustrated by Nils Hogner. Thomas Nelson Sons, New York.
1937.

Holmes, Mabel   *The Lion Dog through the Looking-glass.*
North Arlington, Illinois, U.S.A. 1965.

Hopkins, Lydia et al.   *The Pekingese.*
A Symposium. 113 pp. Field Fancy Publishing Corporation, New
York. 1924.

Howe, E. & E.   *Pekingese Scrapbook.*
132 pp. Chapman & Hall, London. 1954.

Hubbard, C.L.B. *The Pekingese Handbook.*
132 pp. Nicholson & Watson, London. 1951.

Ironside, Margaret *Lung Chung.*
Diplomacy of a Pekingese. 112 pp. Illustrated by Ronald Ferns. Home and van Thal, London. 1946.

Jacob, Naomi *Prince China*
By Himself but dictated to Naomi Jacob. 158 pp. Hutchinson, London. 1955.

Jeans, Angela *Harry the Peke.*
170 pp. Illustrated by K.F. Barker. A. & C. Black, London. 1936.

Johns, Rowland (Editor) *Our Friend the Pekingese.*
86 pp. Methuen & Company, London. 1932.

Johnson, Burges *Sonnets from the Pekingese and other doggerel.*
38 pp. Illustrated by "Edwina". The Macmillan Company, New York. 1935.

Katz, Rose Marie *This is the Pekingese.*
256 pp. T.F.H. Publications, New Jersey, U.S.A. 1962.

King, Louise W. *A Pekingese Keepsake.*
41 pp. Lapin Enterprises, Washington, U.S.A. 1979.
A Pekingese Trifle. 50 pp. Illustrations by Cherie williamson Rush. Lapin Enterprises as above. 1979.
Geronimo and Geranium. The Tale of two Pekingese puppies. Illustrated by Cherie Williamson Rush. 27 pp Lapin Enterprises as above. 1979.

Krieger, Grace A. *Pet Pekingese.*
64 pp. Limited edition of 500 copies. Fond du Lac, Wisconsin, U.S.A. 1954.

Lansdowne, Charmian *The Imperial Dog of China, the Pekingese.*
163 pp. Privately printed 1934. U.S.A.

Lathrop, Dorothy P. *Puppies for Keeps.*
Illustrations by the author. The Macmillan Company, New York. 1943.
The Skittle Skattle Monkey. 40 pp. Illustrations by the author. The Macmillan Company, New York. 1945.
Puffy and the Seven Leaf Clover. 34 pp. Illustrations by the author. The Macmillan Company, New York. 1954.

Leask, Estelle *Pekie Poems by Wo Hoo Git.*
49 pp. New York. 1924.

Legl-Jacobsson, Elisabeth   *East Asiatic Breeds.*
Includes the Pekingese, Truck Produktions, Sweden. 1978.

Quigley, Dorothy A.   *The Quigley Book of the Pekingese.*
200 pp. Howell Book House Inc., New York. 1964.

Quirk, Lorna   *Poopah the Pekingese Pup.*
Australia. 1947.

Ramsay, William   *A Dog and his Friends. The Cats, the Rats, the Ravens,*
the "Hoodie" and "Mailie" the wise old ewe.
127 pp. Arrowsmith, Bristol, United Kingdom. 1930.

Raymond-Mallock, L.   *The Up-to-date Pekingese and all other Toy dogs.*
(See General Toy Books)

Romer, Mabel   *A Peke's Pilgrimage.*
43 pp. Illustrated by G.D. Tidmarsh. Palmer, London. 1920.

Scott, Alice   *How to Raise and Train a Pekingese.*
64pp. T.F.H. Publications, New Jersey, U.S.A. 1959.

Scott, John   *Is it poetry? and some remarks on the Pekingese.*
35 pp. Privately printed, United Kingdom. 1937.

Schneider, Earl (Editor)   *Know your Pekingese.*
63 pp. Pet Library, New York. 1966.
Enjoy your Pekingese. 32 pp. Pet Library, New York. 1967.

Sefton, Frances   *The Pekingese Guide.*
250 pp. The pet Library, New York. 1969.

Shaw, Kerry   *Mother never told me.*
Memoirs of Madame Poo, A Peke. California, U.S.A. 1965.

Smythe, Lillian C. ("Lady Betty")   *The Pekingese.*
A Monograph on the Pekingese Dog: Its History and Points. With notes
on breeding, feeding etc. Photographs of famous dogs and directory
of breeders. 108 pp. "The Kennel" (1909) Limited, London. 1909.
The Pekingese. 2nd edition. C 1910. 135 pp.
The Pekingese. 3rd edition. 1912. 163 pp.
The Pekingese. 4th edition. 1914. 272 pp.
The Pekingese. 5th edition. 1917. 308 pp.

Soutar, Andrew   *A Chinaman in Sussex: sly reflections of a wordly Peke.*
127 pp. Hutchinson, London. 1931.

South, Rowland & Walker, Gerry   *The Odd Adventures of Pip the Peke.*
38 pp. 1944.

Stolz, Mary *The Dragons of the Queen.*
47 pp. Illustrated by Edward Francino. Harper & Row, New York and London. 1969.

Taylor, W. Hindley *Success in Pekingese.*
146 pp. Printed 1961. United Kingdom.

Tocagni, Hector *El Perro Pekines.*
137 pp. Editorial Albatross, Buenos Aires. 1975. In Spanish.

Vare, Daniele *The last of the Empresses and the passing from the Old China to the New.*
258 pp. John Murray, London. 1936.

L'Hommedieu, Dorothy K. *Tyke the little mutt.*
63 pp. Illustrated by Margaret Kirmse. Lippincott Company, New York. 1949.

Little, Alicia *Intimate China.*
Included as the source book of *Little Apricot* (quoted in Pekingese Scrapbook). Author was a pioneer of the Pekingese in the United Kingdom. Hutchinson, London. 1899.

Lucas, E.V. *The Pekingese National Anthem.*
7pp. Illustrated by Persis Kirmse. Methuen & Company, London. 1930. *No Nose at the Show.* 43 pp. Illustrated by Persis Kirmse. Methuen & Company, London. 1931.

Lyde, L.W. *The Golden Lady.*
Some memories of the life and death of a little dog. 59 pp. Country Life, London. 1937.

Mackail, Denis *Life with Topsy.*
415 pp. William Heinemann, London. 1942.

Miller, Madeline *Pekingese as Pets.*
31 pp. T.F.H. Publications, New Jersey, U.S.A. 1956.

Muller-Probster, Paula *Der Vernehme Zimmerhund.*
Japan Chin, Palasthund, Toy Spaniel. 114 pp. Nurnberg, Germany. Druck: Chr. Moser. 1929. In German.

Munnings, Violet (Lady) *Black Knight.*
182 pp. Illustrated by Sir Alfred Munnings, KCVO, RA. Cassell Company, London. 1953.

Nicholas, Anna K. & Brearley, Joan M. *The Book of the Pekingese.*
From Palace Dog to the Present Day. 336 pp. T.F.H. Publications, New Jersey, U.S.A. 1975.

Nicholas, Anna K. *The Pekingese.*
A complete Presentation with Illustrations of the Origin, Development, Breeding, Showing, Training, Kennelling, Care and Feeding of this breed. 141 pp. Judy Publishing Company, Chicago, U.S.A. 1939.

Payne, Joan Balfour *Ambrose.*
48 pp. Illustrated by the author. The World's Work (1913) Limited, Kingswood, United Kingdom. 1959.

Pertwee, Roland *Little Doggerels.*
64 pp. Illustrated by Eileen Soper. Herbert Jenkins, London. 1938.

Phoenice, J. *Peke Posy.*
48 pp. Illustrated by Cherie Williamson Rush. Limited edition of 150 hardbound copies. Lapin Enterprises, Washington, U.S.A. 1981.
Peke Posy. 20 pp. Cover portrait only of *Acacia of Buddletown.* Oriel Press Limited, Newcastle-upon-Tyne, United Kingdom. 1967. (1st English edition.)

Pisano, Beverly *Pekingese.*
125 pp. T.F.H. publications, New Jersey, U.S.A. 1981.

Price, Nancy *I had a Comrade Buddy.*
79 pp. Allen & unwin, London. 1944.
Tails and Tales. 135 pp. Dogs owned by the well known actress, but her Pekingese were special to her. Victor Gollancz Ltd, London. 1945.

Verity-Steele, Queenie *The Book on Pekingese.*
133 pp. Privately printed. United Kingdom. 1914.
This book went into a further 12 editions, the later editions published by Dorothy Slater.

Vlasto, J.A. MB. *The Popular Pekingese.*
144 pp. Popular Dogs Publishing Company, London. 1923, and later.
The New Popular Pekingese. With an article on the breed in America by Mrs. Christian Hager. Also including many new photographs and seventeen new and originaal drawings by Charles J. Allport. 255 pp. Popular Dogs Publishing Company, London 1929.

Waring, Jean *The Fluffy Lions*
The Story of Mighty Atom, Poppet and company. 30 pp. Museum Press, London. 1954.

Whitlock, Brand *Little Lion.*
The Story of Mieke. 42pp. D. Appleton Century Company Inc., New York. 1937.

Younghusband, Ethel   *The Surroundings of Fu Hi.*
   158 pp. Tuggall, Beaconsfield, United Kingdom. 1951.

Magazine and Periodicials:

International Dogs. U.S.A.*The Pekingses as compared with the sleeve dog.* by Harry R. Kendall. 1912.

American Kennel Gazette *Where Pekin's dog is Cherished.* By Arthur Frederick Jones. February 28th 1926.

Where Tiny Pekes a-Hunting Go. By Arthur Frederick Jones. January 1st, 1930.

Meridale Glorifies American-bred Pekes. By Arthur Frederick Jones. March 1st, 1931.

A Sturdy Dog is the Pekingese, Lion Dog of China. By Enno Meyer. January 1st, 1934.

The Pekes of Old Pekin. By C. Walter Young, M.D. September 1st, 1936.

The Pekingese Magazine. Bound copy 1919/1920. Edited by Queenie Verity-Steele. First printed for public circulation July 1919. Published monthly. Lewes, Sussex, United Kingdom.

Pomeranian

Denlinger, Milo G.   *The Complete Pomeranian.*
   128 pp. of which 80 are on the breed. Remainder general care. Denlinger's, U.S.A. 1950.

Frazer, Sir James OM, FRS, & Lady Frazer   *Pasha the Pom.*
   The Story of a little dog. 117 pp. Illustrated by H. M. Brook, R.I. Blackie *Sons, London. 1937.*

Harmar, Hilary   *The Pomeranian.*
   120 pp. W. & G. Foyle, London. 1967.

Herrick, Robert   *Little Black Dog.*
   192 pp. Rockwell, Chicago, U.S.A. 1931.

Hicks, G.M. MA.   *The Pomeranian.*
   115 pp. Our Dogs Publishing Company, Manchester, United Kingdom. 1906.

Hughes, Pauline B.   *Your Pomeranian.*
   128 pp. Denlinger's , U.S.A. 1969.

Ives, Lilla   *Show Pomeranians.*
   3rd revised edition. 71 pp. Our Dogs Publishing Company, Manchester, United Kingdom. 1926.

Ives, The late Miss L.   *Show Pomeranians.*
4th edition revised and brought up to date by Mrs. Fred Thomson. 68 pp. Our Dogs, as above. 1929.

Johns, Rowland (Editor)   *Our Friend the Pomeranian.*
88 pp. Methuen Company, London. 1934.

Liebers, Arthur & Sheppard, Mrs. G.   *How to Raise and Train a Pomeranian.*
64 pp. T.F.H. Publications, New Jersey, U.S.A. 1959.

Miller, Evelyn   *Pomeranians as Pets.*
18 pp. T.F.H. Publications, New Jersey, U.S.A. 1958.

Parker, Mrs. E.   *The Popular Pomeranian.*
165 pp. Popular Dogs Publishing Company, London. 1928.

Parker, Mrs. E. & Wilson, Linda A.   *The Popular Pomeranian.*
2nd edition revised. 187 pp. Popular Dogs Publishing Company, London. C 1937.

Ricketts, Viva Leone   *The New Complete Pomeranian.*
261 pp of which 134 pp are on the breed. Remainder general care. Howell Book House Inc., New York. 1962.
The New Complete Pomeranian.
New edition 1965.

Schneider, Earl (Editor)   *Enjoy your Pomeranian.*
32 pp. Pet Library, New York.
Know your Pomeranian. 64 pp. Pet Library, New York.

Spirer, Louise Zeigler Herbert F.   *This is the Pomeranian.*
223 pp. T.F.H. Publications, New Jersey, U.S.A. 1965.
Vic, the autobiography of a Pomeranian Dog (A true story). 1st edition. 92 pp. Manchester, United Kingdom. 1880.

Pug

Brassey, Annie (Lady)   *Voyage in the "Sunbeam".*
United Kingdom. 1878 and later editions.

Brearley, Joan M.   *The Book of the Pug.*
256 pp. T.F.H. Publications, New Jersey, U.S.A. 1980.

Cryer, Dr. M.H.   *The Prize Pugs of America and England.*
151 pp. Fanciers Publishing Company of Philadelphia, U.S.A. 1891.

Daglish, E. Fitch   *Pugs.*
90 pp. W. & G. Foyle, London. 1962.

Denlinger, Milo G.   *The Complete Pug.*
125 pp. of which 61 are on the breed. Remainder general care. Denlinger's, U.S.A. 1947.

Doherty, Filomena   *Pet Pug.*
64 pp. Illustrated by Gladys Emerson Cook. All-Pets, Fond du Lac, Wisconsin, U.S.A. 1956.

Featherstone, G.   *Pug Dog Miscellany.*
65 pp. Privately printed, United Kingdom. C 1950.
A Thesis on the origin of the Pug Dog. 4 pages of typescript. Privately printed, United Kingdom, C 1952.

Gordon, John F.   *The Pug.*
100 pp. John Gifford, London. 1973.

Hurry, C.   *The Oracle Dog and the Sages.*
29 pp. Illustrated by Michael Lewis. Written in the style of a legend. Nicol Books, London. 1954.

Lockhart, Marian   *Three Curly Tails and others.*
60 pp. Illustrated by W. Dacres Adams. Bickers & Sons Limited, Kondon. 1909.

Miller, Evelyn   *Pugs as Pets.*
18pp. T.F.H. Publications, New Jersey, U.S.A. 1959. How to Raise and Train a Pug. 64 pp. T.F.H. Publications, New Jersey, U.S.A. 1960.

Pisano, Beverly   *Pugs*
125 pp. T.F.H. Publications, New Jersey, U.S.A. 1981.

Pug Dog Club of America   *A Celebration of Pugs.*
1885 - 1985. 306 pp. (Spiral bound). Pug Dog Club of America 1985.

Pughe, L.J.E.   *Black Pugs.*
Hints on their Management. J.   G. Toulmin, Blackburn. United Kingdom. 1905.

Rowntree, Harry   *The Adventures of the Black Pug.*
C 1915.

Schneider, Earl (Editor)   *Know your Pug.*
64 pp. The Pet Library, New York.

Spirer, Louise Zeigler & Herbert F.   *This is the Pug.*
223 pp. T.F.H. Publications, New Jersey, U.S.A. 1968.

Swainston-Goodger, W.   *The Pug-Dog.*
Its History and Origin. 95 pp. Watmoughs, Idle and London. 1930.
The Truth About the Pug Dog. Pamphlet of 12 pp. in blue wrappers with photograph. Privately printed. United Kingdom. 1947.

IMPORTANT AND INTERESTING TOYS

The coming of women into the hobby and business of dog breeding had a marked effect upon the breeds. Between them they evolved and greatly improved many of the most attractive types, such as the Papillon, the Griffon, the Pekingese and the Pug, of which examples are shown here. The Papillon is Mrs. F. A. Pope's "Gay Buchaneer," the embodiment of active health. On the right is Mrs. Parker Rhodes's Griffon, Ch. "Precious." Lower left the Pekingese, Miss Heuston's Ch. "T'ouen." Lastly, the black Pug, Miss Voy's Ch. "Peter of Inver." When such dogs as these are compared with the old type the improvement is astounding, they are sometimes hardly recognizable as the same breeds Published **1930's**

AN EARLY DOG SHOW

When dog shows were yet young, they were considered exciting. Newspaper reporters were chosen for their courage rather than from any literary ability or reporting energy. This picture shows the arrival of "Idstone," with his Irish setters and the Rev. .... "T... d unless I am mistaken the noted Mastiff "Crown Prince." In the dim background are two lady

The Pug Handbook. 132 pp. Nicholson & Watson, London. 1959.

Trullinger, J.W. et al. *The Complete Pug.*
New revised edition. 272 pp. Howell Book House Inc., New York.
1972.

Veldhuis, Christina *Der Mops.*
(The Pug) Rudolf Muller, Koln, Germany. 1985. In German.

Weall, Susan Graham *The Pug.*
159 pp. Popular Dogs, London. 1965.

Wolf, Esther E. *Your Pug.*
128 pp. Denlinger's, U.S.A. 1972.

Worth, Valerie *Curlicues.*
The Fortunes of two Pug Dogs. 51 pp. Illustrated by Natalie Babbitt.
Farran-Straus Giroux, New York. 1980.

Yorkshire Terrier

Brearley, Joan M. *The Book of the Yorkshire Terrier.*
352 pp. T.F. H. Publications, New Jersey, U.S.A. 1984.

Brewster, Mary S. *Yorkshire Terrier Champions. 1971- 1974.*
Montvale, New Jersey, U.S.A. 1974.

Bulgin, Gwen *The Yorkshire Terrier.*
96 pp. John Bartholomew & Sons, Edinburgh. 1977.

Callender, Richard *I'm Nick.*
A Yorkshire Terrier's Story. 199 pp. Illustrated by Frank Adams. W. T.
Chambers, London. 1934.

Donnelly, Kerry *Know your Yorkshire Terrier.*
125 pp. T.F.H. Publications, New Jersey, U.S.A. 1979.

Glenn, Patricia *Your Baby, the Yorkshire Terrier Puppy.*
107 pp. Vantage Press, New York. 1975.

Gold, Fay *The Story of Goldie V. Stone, and the Petite Kennels.*
Fay Gold Publications, New York. 1967.

Louie. The Story of a Yorkshire Terrier. 18 pp. Photographs and line
drawings. Published as above. 1970.

Training your Yorkshire Terrier. A Manual for the Novice. 42pp.
Published as above. 1974.

Gordon, J.B. & Bennett, J. E. *The Complete Yorkshire Terrier.*
319 pp. Howell Book House Inc., New York. 1977.

Howard, Morris *Your Yorkshire Terrier.*
128 pp. Denlinger's, U.S.A. 1972.

Huxham, Mona *All About the Yorkshire Terrier.*
191 pp. Pelham Books, London. 1971.

Jessop Sam *The Yorkshire Terrier.*
Rev. edition. 34 pp. Our Dogs Publishing Company, Manchester. C.1908.

Liebers, Arthur & Miller, D. *How to Raise and Train a Yorkshire Terrier.*
64 pp. T.F.H. Publications, New Jersey, U.S.A. 1959.

Little, Mildred S. *Susie, little friend.*
(The true story of a little dog). 44pp. Pitman, London. n.d.

Martello, Aileen M. *The Yorkshire Terrier.*
106 pp. Illustrated by Anne Reitz Holt. Origin, History and complete care. Exposition Press, New York. 1971.

Migliorini, Mario *Yorkshire Terriers.*
76 pp. Arco Pet Library, New York. 1971.

Miller, Evelyn *Yorkshire Terriers as Pets.*
26 pp. T.F.H. Publications, New Jersey, U.S.A. 1958.

Montgomeryp-Campbell, M. *The Chronicles of Baba.*
A Canine Teetotum. 253 pp. Jarrold & Sons, London. 1900.

Munday, Ethel *The Popular Yorkshire Terrier.*
160 pp. Popular dogs, London. 1958.
The Yorkshire Terrier. 166 pp. Popular Dogs, London. 1966.

Nathan, Robert *Journey of Tapiola.*
102 pp. Constable, London. 1938.
Tapiola's Brave Regiment. 137 pp. Illustrated by Kurt Wiese. Alfred A. Knopf, New York. 1941.
The Adventures of Tapiola. Alfred A. Knopf, New York. 1950.

Pata, Jan Linzy *Yorkshire Terrier Champions. 1952-1980.*
214 pp. Pata Publications, California, U.S.A. 1982.

Phelps, Elizabeth Stuart *Loveliness.*
Short story of a Yorkshire Terrier. 43 pp. Illustrated by Sarah S. Stilwell. Houghton Mifflin, boston, U.S.A. 1899.

Sameja, O. *The Yorkshire Terrier. Its Care and Training.*
97 pp. K. & R. Books, Edlington, Lincolnshire, United Kingdom. 1978.

Schneider, Earl (Editor) *Know your Yorkshire Terrier.*
64pp. Pet Library, New York. n.d.

Sloane, Julia M. *The Diary of Two Red Cross Dogs.*
22 pp. Privately printed 1917. Pasadena, U.S.A.

Swan, Annie   *The Yorkshire Terrier Handbook.*
    123 pp. Nicholson & Watson, London. 1958.
Whitehead, Colonel H.F.   *Yorkshire Terrier.*
    77 pp. W. & G. Foyle, London. 1961.

Titles referred to in this book.

American Kennel Club Stud Book. U.S.A. 1886.

American Kennel Club's   *World of the Pure-bred Dog.*
    U.S.A. 1985.

Ash, Edward C.   *Dogs: Their History and Development.*
    Ernest Benn Ltd., London. 1927.
    The Pekingese. Cassell & Company, London. 1936.

Bagshaw, Margaret R.   *Pet Miniature Pinscher.*
    All-Pets Books Inc., Wisconsin, U.S.A. 1958.

Berjeau, Ph. Charles   *The Varieties of Dogs as they are found
                    in Old Sculptures, Pictures, Engravings and Books.*
    Dulau & Company, London. 1863.

Berners, J.   *The Boke of St. Albans.*
    1486 and 1881.

Bewick, Thomas   *History of Quadrupeds.*
    Edward Walter, T. Bewick & S. Hodgson, Newcastle-upon-Tyne. 1807.

Brassey, Lady   *Voyage of the Sunbeam.*
    1878.

Brown, Captain Thomas   *Biographical Sketches and Authentic Anecdotes
    ERSE, FLS, MRPSE, MWS.   of Dogs*
    Simpkin & Marshall, London. 1829.

Bruette, Dr. William A. & Donnelly, Kerry V.   *The Original Complete
                                            Dog Book*
    TFH Publications, U.S.A. 1979.

Caius, Dr. J.   *De Canibus Britannicis.*
    1570.

Callender, Richard   *I'm Nick.*
    W. & T. Chambers Limited, London. 1934.

Cardew, Mirri   *A Chinese Crested Dog for Me.*
    Midland Counties Publications, Leicester. 1986.

Katherine   *With the Empress Dowager of China.*
The New Century Company, New York. 1906.

Casselli, R. et al.   *The Complete Chihuahua.*
Howell Book House Inc., U.S.A. 1967.

Compton, Herbert, (Editor)   *The Twentieth Century Dog.*
Grant Richards, London. 1904.

Cousens, M.   *Griffon Bruxellois.*
W. & G. Foyle, London. 1960.

Coventry, Francis   *The History of Pompey the Little.*
London. 1735.

de Bylandt, Count Henri   *Dogs of All Nations.*
Kegan Paul, Trench, Trubner & Company, London. 1905.

Dalziel, Hugh ("Corsincon")   *British Dogs.*
Upcott Gill, London. 1879/1880.

Davis, Henry P. (Editor)   *The Modern Dog Encyclopaedia.*
Stackpole & Heck Inc., U.S.A. 1949.

Dempsey, Dixie   *The Complete Toy Manchester.*
Denlinger's, U.S.A. 1950.

Fisher, H.A.L. PC., DCL., FBA., FRS.   *A History of Europe.*
Edward Arnold & Company, London. 1938.

Fountain, R. & Gates A.   *Stubb's Dogs.*
Ackermann, London. 1984.

Godden Rumer   *The Butterfly Lions.*
Macmillan (London) Limited. 1977.

Hamilton-Smith, Lieut. Col. C.   *Dogs*
1839/1840 (Vols IX & X of Sir William Jardine's Naturalist's Library)
London.

Harmar, Hilary   *Chihuahuas.*
W. & G. Foyle, London. 1966.
The Complete Chihuahua Encyclopaedia. Arco Publishing Company, Inc. New York. 1972.

Hick, G.M. MA   *The Pomeranian.*
Our Dogs Publishing Company, Manchester. 1906.

Houtart, Baron Albert   *Les Epagneuls Nains Continentaux.*
Chasse et Pêche, Brussels. 1925.

Hubbard C.L.B. (Editor)   *The Observer's Book of Dogs.*
Frederick Warne & Company, London. 1945.

Hutchinsons *Illustrated Dog Encyclopaedia.*
London. 1935.

Iveria, Miki *Maltese Dogs: The Jewels of Women.*
The Maltese Club of Great Britain. 1979.

Jaquet, E.W. *The Kennel Club, A History & Record of its Work.*
The Kennel Gazette, London. 1905.

Kennel, The *Ladies' Kennel Journal.*
London. 1896.

Lane, Charles H. *Dog Shows and Doggy People.*
Hutchinson & Company, London. 1902.

Lathrop, Dorothy *The Dog in the Tapestry Garden.*
Macmillan & Company, New York. 1962.

Lee, Rawdon B. *A History and Description of Modern Dogs.*
Horace Cox, London. 1894.

Leitch, Virginia T. *The Maltese Dog.*
Jon Vir Kennels, Maryland, U.S.A. 1953.

Leighton, Robert *The New Book of the Dog.*
Cassell & Company, London. 1912.
The Complete Book of the Dog. Cassell & Company, London. 1922.

Li Ching-fong, His Excellency Lord *The Pekingese 1912.*
L.C. Smythe, West Kensington, London.

Lockhart, Marion *Three Curly Tails and Others.*
Bickers & Sons Limited, London. 1909.

Lytton, The Hon. Mrs. Neville *Toy Dogs and their Ancestors.*
Duckworth, London. 1911.

Martello, Aileen M. *The Yorkshire Terrier.*
Exposition Press Inc., New York. 1971.

Meyrick, John *House Dogs and Sporting Dogs.*
John van Voorst, London. 1861.

Milner, Ada *Les Chiens d'Agrément.*
Privately published, Paris. 1924..

Montgomery-Campbell, M. *The Chronicles of Baba.*
Jarrold & Sons, London. 1901.

Murray, T. Douglas. *The Ancient Palace Dogs of China (The Pekingese) 1909)*

Nathan, Robert *I'm Nick.*
W. & R. Chambers, London. 1934.

Oliver, Annette   *Living with Italian Greyhounds.*
Privately published. 1983.

Pearce, Thomas ("Idstone")   *The Dog*
Cassell, Petter & Galpin, London, 1845.

"Pall Mall Gazette"   *Pets of the Boudoir.*
1886.

Ransome, Arthur   *The Coot Club*
Jonathan Cape, London, 1934.

Ransom, J.   *The Dog Directory Guide to the Bichon Frisè*
Dog Directory, Bracknell, Berkshire, United Kingdom, 1978.

Raynham, L.C. (Doone)   *The History and Management of the*
Griffon Bruxellois.
Scan Books, Brighton, United Kingdom, 1985.

Richardson, H.D.   *Dogs, their Origins and Varieties.*
James McGlashhan, Dublin. 1851.

Ricketts, Viva Leone   *The Complete Miniature Pinscher*
Howell Book House, U.S.A., 1972.

Russell Allen, M. Diana ("Mard")   *Little Cupid.*
n.d. Privately published.

Seebohm, Henry   *Siberia in Europe.*

Sefton, Frances   *Pekingese Guide.*
Pet Library, New York. 1969.

Shaw, Vero, B.A. (Cantab.)   *The Illustrated Book of the Dog.*
Cassell & Company, London. 1879/1881.

Spicer, Mrs. M. Handley   *Toy Dogs and How to Breed and Rear Them.*
Adam & Charles Black, London. 1902.

Stenning, Eilidh   *Cavalier King Charles Spaniels.*
W. & G. Foyle, London. 1964.

Sully   *A Popular History of France.*
(Historian and Minister to King Henri III)

Swainston-Goodger, W.   *The Pug Dog.*
Watmough's, Idle and London. 1930.

Taplin, William   *The Sportsman's Cabinet.*
J. Cundee, London. 1803/1804.

The Terrier Magazine, 1948.

Thornhill, R.B.   *The Shooting Directory.*
Longman Hurst, Rees & Orme, London. 1804.

Townesend, Stephen, FRCS *A Thoroughbred Mongrel.*
T. Fisher Unwin, London. 1900.

Tracy, Julia Lowndes *Terrier V.C.*
Aldine Publishing Company Limited, London. c1915.

Vesey-Fitzgerald, B. *The Book of the Dog.*
Nicholson & Watson, London. 1948.

Walsh, J.H. ("Stonehenge") *Dogs of the British Islands.*
Horace Cox, London. 1867, 1878.

The Dog In Health & Disease. Longmans, Green, Reader and Dyer.
London. 1867.

Warner Hill, Frank *Dog World.*
(Article). 2nd January 1976.

Watson, James *The Dog Book*
William Heinemann, London. 1906.

Country Life in America (Magazine). 1914.

Waud, Clarice & Hutchings, M.W. *The Papillon 'Butterfly' Dog*
Fancier's Supplies, Liss, Hampshire. 1985.

INDEX

A

B

D

I

Q

R

S